Age and Sex in Human Societies:
A Biosocial Perspective

Age and Sex in Human Societies:
A Biosocial Perspective

Pierre L. van den Berghe
UNIVERSITY OF WASHINGTON

WADSWORTH PUBLISHING COMPANY, INC.
BELMONT, CALIFORNIA

HM
131
.V23
1973

© 1973 by Wadsworth Publishing Company, Inc., Belmont, California 94002. All rights reserved. No part of this book may be reproduced, stored in a retrieval system or transcribed, in any form or by any means, electronic, mechanical, photocopying, recording, or otherwise, without the prior written permission of the publisher.

ISBN: 0-534-00311-7

L. C. Cat. Card No. 73-88811

Printed in the United States of America

1 2 3 4 5 6 7 8 9 10---76 75 74 73

To keep the price of this book as low as possible, we have used an economical means of typesetting. We welcome your comments.

Acknowledgments

My first and most long-lasting debt in the development of this book is to my wife, Irmgard, and my sons, Eric and Oliver. By constituting, together with me, the simplest possible form of an age and sex differentiated society, they provided me with a constant source of insights.

A number of my colleagues read and criticized various parts of the manuscript; I should especially like to thank Robert Burgess and Edward Gross at the University of Washington, John Finley Scott at the University of California at Davis, Hans Kummer at the University of Zürich, Aubrey Manning and Tom Burns at the University of Edinburgh, and Lionel Tiger of the Guggenheim Foundation. Last but not least, Beulah Reddaway typed the manuscript with her customary efficiency.

Preface

Books do not simply happen. They have a life history. They have an instant of conception, a protracted gestation (during which their authors are often moody and disagreeable), an initiation ritual when the publisher releases them on the market, a period of vitality when they are read, a phase of senescence when they become obsolete, and, in the end, a decent burial on the shelves of libraries. Unlike biological organisms, however, their life span varies greatly, they reproduce asexually, and a precious few achieve something close to immortality, at least on the human temporal scale.

Organic analogies are facile, and their abuse in the early phases of social science has laid them to rest for several decades. My use of one here is deliberate. The organic skeleton in the social science closet is beginning to rattle too audibly to be ignored much longer.

Why did I write this book? The immediate occasion was a new sociology course on Age and Sex Differentiation which I offered to teach in 1970 and actually did teach in 1972. My offering to teach the course was directly stimulated by a course proposal on the "Sociology of Sex Differentiation" presented by a Women's Caucus of sociology graduate students. This proposal was one of a dozen or so presented by feminist groups on campus, which offered courses dealing with such topics as "The Economics of Sexual Discrimination," "Women in Literature," "Herstory," and others. The political climate was obviously ripe for this kind of course, and, indeed, a number of such courses were offered in Winter and Spring of 1971, as a kind of embryonic Women's Studies Program, analogous to the currently popular black and ethnic studies.

My own reaction to the course proposal on the "Sociology of Sex Differentiation" was that the topic had been sadly neglected in our sociology curriculum, although it was basic to our discipline. For years, I had been teaching a course entitled "Social Differentiation," in which, after devoting one week each to age and sex differentiation, I proceeded to deal with social stratification in the more conventional sense. That course always left me frustrated because I felt that I was not giving age and sex the places they obviously deserved in our understanding of human societies. I sensed that the subjects of age and sex, both rooted in biology, would inevitably raise fundamental and conveniently sidestepped issues concerning the determinants of human behavior; I felt, furthermore, that age and sex were so closely linked to each other as to dictate their being treated jointly.

Although I agreed with the Women's Caucus's diagnosis of the position of women in society and with its condemnation of sex discrimination, I also strongly disagreed with the intellectual, ideological, and tactical positions of several of its members. First, I disagreed with the separatist premise, adapted from the model of black and ethnic studies, that the study of women was a distinct topic that could be meaningfully divorced from the study of men, and that could best be taught by women to women. Female separatism seems even less a viable alternative than does black separatism. Consciousness-raising and identity-searching were one thing; teaching an undergraduate sociology course as I conceived of it, quite another.

Second, I was disturbed by the test of ideological conformity that the Women's Caucus applied in evaluating the contribution of a course or an instructor. In particular, I considered the attempt to stigmatize as "sexist" any serious consideration of the biological components of human behavior to be anti-intellectual. I felt that the topic of sex differentiation, to be done justice to, necessarily required at least a minimum of familiarity with the anthropological, primatological, ethological, and human biological literature.

To be sure, some of that literature was also relatively new to me, but I was willing to look at it and to try to evaluate its relevance without being limited by any organized group's party line. I, therefore, presented an alternative course proposal that became incorporated into the sociology curriculum at the university, and which developed into the present book. The validity of my concern for the preservation of intellectual freedom was quickly vindicated. No sooner was my course established, than the Women's Caucus demanded of the chairman of the department that I be prevented from teaching it. In the end, both courses were offered, mine in the Sociology Department, the Women's Caucus's in the General Studies Program, a happy solution which allowed students a free choice of intellectual fare.

The reason that I mention these political antecedents to the genesis of this book is emphatically *not* that I wish to

claim for myself Olympian detachment and objectivity and to
stigmatize my protagonists for lacking these qualities. I
firmly believe that social science is inevitably linked with
ideology and politics; therefore, I am convinced that honesty
requires one to reveal the political context of one's intellectual stance. The most that I can claim is that I try not
to let my thinking be shaped by whether it is apt to please
any particular person or group. Of course, this is not to say
that my position is not profoundly shaped by my personal prejudices and experiences. Indeed, it is, and I do not pretend
otherwise.

Contents

INTRODUCTION 1

Chapter 1 AGE AND SEX IN EVOLUTIONARY PERSPECTIVE 6

    Trends toward increasing gender differentiation, infant dependency, longevity, and toward decreasing fertility and infant mortality as organisms become more complex.

Chapter 2 AGE AND SEX AMONG PRIMATES 11

    What does primatology teach us about the range of behavior shown by sub-human primates in captivity and in the wild? Sexual dimorphism, male dominance, and age differentiation among primates, especially the great apes (gibbon, orangutan, gorilla, chimpanzee) and the terrestrial Old World monkeys (baboons, macaques).

Chapter 3 THE HUMAN BIOLOGY OF AGE AND SEX 33

    What is the relevance of biology to an understanding of human behavior? The physiology of maturation and aging. The effect of age on mental abilities. The physiology of sex. Sexual dimorphism, hormones, sex-linked genes. Hermaphroditism. Genetic, hormonal and gonadal sex. Gender differences in character and abilities.

Chapter 4 SEX DIFFERENTIATION IN HUMAN SOCIETIES 52

    Sex and the division of labor: cross-cultural similarities and differences. Socialization and sex roles.

Transvestism and homosexuality. The universality of
male dominance. Three case studies: Tuareg, Hausa,
Yoruba. The status of women in relation to the rule
of descent, the rule of residence, polygyny versus
monogamy, the role of women in economic production,
and the level of technology.

Chapter 5   AGE DIFFERENTIATION IN HUMAN SOCIETIES   74

The universality of age differentiation. Rites of
passage. Age grades and age sets. Relative versus
absolute age. Sociological versus chronological age.
Age, generation, and the kinship system. Age as a
form of stratification. Age distinctions and technology. Seniority and unilineal descent. Primogeniture.
East African age-set societies. The Masai.

Chapter 6   THE DYNAMICS OF AGE AND SEX CONFLICTS   89

The relationship between age and sex differentiation.
The tyranny of adult males. Sex and age conflicts.
The family as a micro-tyranny. Marriage as a basis
of female subordination. Age, sex, and other bases
of inequality. Technology and age and sex inequalities. Stratification, endogamy, exogamy, and hypergamy. The Freudian interpretation of generation
conflicts. Rituals of rebellion. Hazing, mock combat, and humor as ritualized modes of expressing age
and sex conflicts. Age, sex, and revolution.

Chapter 7   INDUSTRIAL SOCIETIES   104

The effect of industrial technology on age and sex
roles. Ideology and the feminist movement. Feminism
and abolitionism. Capitalism versus socialism. Trends
in sex segregation in occupations. Sexism, racism, and
other forms of exploitation. The family as the source
of sex inequality. Industrialization and age inequalities. Age segregation. The elderly as an underprivileged group. The youth movement. Prospects for change.

GLOSSARY   121

BIBLIOGRAPHY   124

INDEX   137

Introduction

The relative neglect of age and sex differentiation in sociology (and to a lesser extent in anthropology) is in no small measure, I think, ascribable to the fact that age and sex differences are rooted in morphology and physiology. Their relevance to the social sciences lies in the fact that, although partly biologically determined, age and sex differences feature prominently in the structure of all human societies. Some phenomena seem to be uniquely (or nearly uniquely) human, but universal within the species of *Homo sapiens*. All socialized humans, for example, have highly developed, learned, vocalized, articulated, symbolic systems that they use for communication and the transmission of culture, but even the "languages" of the great apes only remotely approach the complexity of human speech. A second group of phenomena are not universally human but are found only in humans. Not all, but *only* human societies, for example, print money, use the wheel, or have prostitutes. These two classes of phenomena are clearly within the province of the social sciences.

Still another set of phenomena are clearly physical, and are shared by man and other species, but have only minimal bearing on man's social behavior. For example, the fact that we breathe oxygen or burn calories does not condition our social behavior, beyond placing limits on our natural habitat and the extent to which we can pollute it. These phenomena, then, belong in the natural sciences.

Age and sex differentiation, on the other hand, are clearly marginal phenomena, being a fundamental feature of numerous human *and* nonhuman societies. In human societies, both the *social elaboration* and the *biological basis* of age and sex differentiation are crucial. An understanding of age and sex in humans thus requires not only a cross-cultural approach, but also a cross-specific one, that is, one that compares different biological species. More fundamentally, age and sex differences in man reopen the issue of the biological determination of human behavior, an issue so long brushed aside in the social sciences, and only recently under massive reexamination. As Tiger and Fox (1971) urgently stress, it is high time that we seriously look at ourselves as merely one biological species among many.

From about 1930 to 1970, the mainstream of the social sciences in Europe and North America was strongly environmentalist, and almost as strongly antievolutionary. There were several reasons for these biases. The crude applications of Darwinian and eugenic ideas to human societies, fashionable in the late nineteenth and early twentieth centuries, became increasingly untenable in the light of the accumulating evidence from anthropology, archaeology, paleontology, and linguistics. Human evolution, it turned out, was far more complex than the early social scientists had dreamt, and also very different from biological evolution. In addition, these crude theories of genetic determinism were too embarrassingly linked to the racist and elitist ideologies that buttressed the interests of the ruling classes of capitalist societies. The early schemes of unilinear social evolution (that all societies passed through all the same evolutionary stages) proved far too simplistic as our knowledge of non-Western societies increased. Finally, social scientists, in marking their territory against the competing (and, on the whole, far better established) claims of biological and physical scientists, had an obvious stake in asserting the unique status of *Homo sapiens*, and the radical discontinuity between his behavior and that of "lower organisms."

The most fundamental article of faith in the social scientists' credo was that human behavior is overwhelmingly more *autodeterministic* (man consciously shapes his actions) than that of even his biological next-of-kin, the great apes. The "missing links" had obligingly vanished from circulation, reappearing only as an occasional tooth or skull cap fragment dug up at extravagant expense by paleontologists, but mercifully silent and inert. The fundamental humanity of man was that he consciously transmitted his infinitely plastic and uniquely self-made culture and shaped his own destiny by creating societies out of human interaction itself. Man created God; and the social scientist, being clearly more perspicaceous than his fellows, told the rest of his species that God was really Society, or in the last analysis, Man himself, and that there was no need for false modesty in the scientific scheme of things. Man's unique and seemingly inexhaustible capacity to exploit his fellow men and make them feel miserable became a dominant theme in the Marxian social science tradition, but was conveniently glossed over in the functionalist school that dominated the Anglo-Saxon countries in which the social sciences were most developed.

3 Introduction

Naturally, one of the main emphases in social science was on the almost limitless plasticity of human behavior, at least in all the truly human things that really count: speech, religion, political systems, cosmologies, and so on. The 1930s, 1940s, and 1950s saw the triumph of anthropological relativism and its gradual spread to the hitherto more ethnocentric disciplines of sociology, political science, and economics. In psychology, behaviorism stressed the importance of learning, and in this basic respect was congruent with the sociocultural determinism of sociologists and anthropologists. Human behavior was basically learned through the rewards and punishments dispensed by other humans. "Universals" in human societies were held to be few, and even these few universals were frequently explained through ingenious functional theories of cultural determinism. Thus, the universality of the nuclear family, for example, has generated a prolific literature on the incest taboo as the primordial human invention, the sublime passage from nature to culture, the act of divine creation in the anthropological Book of Genesis. Man ceased to be a beast by self-imposed restrictions on mating. He created larger societies by forcing himself to find mates outside the family into which he was born.

A corollary of this glorification of man, of the rejection of the crude nineteenth-century racism, and of the spread of egalitarian ideologies, is that, since *Homo sapiens* constitutes a single biological superspecies, then all human societies are equally worthy of admiration, each in its own terms. Vastly different though human societies are in technology, size, political centralization, productivity, language, religion, kinship structure, and so on, all are admirable in their humanity. True, an anthropologist may have safely decried the war in Vietnam, Nazi concentration camps, American slavery, and a few other selected barbarities committed in his own or closely related societies, but let him attack head hunting, female infanticide, foot binding, cannibalism, widow suicide, witch hunting, clitoridectomy, or any of the more exotic forms of cruelty, and he runs the serious risk of being exposed as an ethnocentric boor by a distinguished colleague who will promptly find a very good functional explanation for the phenomenon in question. An anthropologist, for example, may with impunity defend cannibalism as a significant source of protein or female infanticide as an effective population control device, but let the same anthropologist suggest that the Nazi genocide of the Jews was an effective mechanism to reinforce the solidarity of the German nation in a difficult period, and he will be stigmatized as a fascist. Perhaps I should confess my own bias: I believe that most human societies are fairly rotten, though each in its creatively unique way; technology enables man to increase the scale, but scarcely the depth, of his beastliness.

Beastliness brings us directly to the topic of age and sex differentiation. All human societies are differentiated *at least* on the basis of age and sex, and, as is the case with many other bases of differentiation, the difference is always to some extent invidious. Defining power as the ability to enforce one's will despite resistance, and tyranny as the gratuitous use of power (that is, the use of power as its own reward rather than simply a means to an end), then all human societies are tyrannical on the two dimensions of age and sex, and most societies on additional dimensions as well. Indeed, the number of dimensions on which societies are tyrannical is a good measure of their scale and complexity of social organization, and is an important correlate of social evolution. The simplest and most universal model for tyranny is the nuclear family, which combines in purest form both sex and age differentiation. The nuclear family is the microtyranny par excellence.

These provocative statements need, of course, to be qualified. Not all societies are equally tyrannical in respect to age and sex, nor are age and sex differentiation purely and simply reducible to the tyranny of men over women and adults over children. For example, the family provides such positive conditions as nurturing for the young; it shares resources, and protects females and infants. If these and many other qualifications did not have to be made, this book could stop here.

Now is probably the best time to confess to a second personal bias. While, clearly, not all human relationships are reducible to the power dimension, I believe that relations of power are the best single starting point in understanding the structure of any society. Quite apart from the complicated question of causal sequences (for example, which comes first: differential relations of power or differential relations of production?), power differentials often have readily observable behavioral consequences. If nothing else, power asymmetries are often glaringly obvious, and much of the basic structure of a society is defined by networks of asymmetrical relationships. For this reason, the dominance-submission component of both age and sex differentiation will loom large in the forthcoming analysis, and so will the group conflicts that inequalities almost inevitably generate in human societies. In this respect, my treatment of the topic will be at variance with the "division of labor" approach to the topic first popularized in sociology by Durkheim and since enshrined in most "Marriage and the Family" textbooks. More than enough has been said by sociologists about how nice and useful an institution the family is. I propose, therefore, to take up again the profound insight of Marx and Engels that the family is an institution ideally suited to the exploitation of women and children. In Engels' words (1942), "the first class oppression [coincides] with that of the female sex by the male"; or, as August Bebel stated, "Woman was a slave before the slave existed."

5   Introduction

    The whole issue of the linkage between power and age and sex differentiation has been raised by Tiger and Fox (1971). Citing as evidence the hierarchical and male-dominated character of savannah-dwelling terrestrial primates, they suggest that the urge to dominate is part of the human "biogram," or inherited behavioral predispositions. Politics, they say, are ultimately a question of genetics, since there is a close relationship between a male primate's dominance and his ability to reproduce. Lust for power is thus a biologically programmed lust for reproduction. Whether or not one accepts the implicit functionalism of the Tiger and Fox argument, the fact remains that all human societies are stratified at least by age and sex, and that the simplest form of social organization, the family, is the prototypical age and sex hierarchy.

    In the last decade or so, the intellectual pendulum in the social sciences has begun to swing away from extreme environmentalism and toward genetic determinism. What Tiger and Fox (1966) have termed the *zoological perspective* on human behavior has taken many forms, from the neoracism of Hensen (1969) concerning innate differences in types of intelligence between whites and blacks in America, to the theories of Ardrey (1961) on the predatory origins of man, the killer-ape. The earlier glorification of man is currently yielding to his vilification.

    If there was any attempt in the previous generation of social scientists to qualify the abrupt transition from nature to culture, it was in the direction of humanizing animals: some animals, we were told, had at least the rudiments of a transmitted culture, used tools, and communicated through perhaps not entirely instinctual languages. Now the trend is to bestialize man. In the end, Konrad Lorenz may well have been closest to the truth when he suggested that "the missing link between the apes and *Homo sapiens* is man." Or in Blaise Pascal's words: "*L'homme n'est ni ange ni bête, mais le malheur veut que qui veut faire l'ange fait la bête.*"[1] The present work will endeavor to place man both in nature and in culture.

---

    [1]"Man is neither angel nor brute, and the misfortune is that he who would act the angel acts the brute" (*Pensées*, 1670, Sect. VI, No. 358).

1 Age and Sex in Evolutionary Perspective

In evolutionary perspective, several general trends in age and sex are apparent among animals. First, sexual differentiation appears fairly early since the great majority of multicellular organisms and all vertebrates have discrete male and female sexes. Second, the more complex and developed the organism is, the closer and more direct the sexual act required for reproduction. Third, as organisms become more complex, the dependence of the young on the adults increases both in length of time and in degree. Fourth, the number of offspring per adult tends to decrease with biological complexity and size. Fifth, infant mortality decreases steeply as one goes up the evolutionary scale. Sixth, the complexity of organisms and their longevity tend to be closely related. All of these trends have profound implications for our topic and need to be at least briefly illustrated.

Regarding sexual differentiation, monocellular organisms generally reproduce by *mitosis*—a process whereby the cell nucleus duplicates itself and splits the cell into two like cells. Barring accidental death, monocellular organisms thus achieve an immortality of sorts. Many other organisms, including plants and invertebrates, such as worms, mollusks, sponges, and barnacles achieve sexual differentiation, but the same individual organism carries both sexes. This phenomenon is known as *hermaphroditism*. Among insects, arachnids, and other invertebrates, the two sexes are generally carried by distinct animals, though sometimes the sex of the individual is determined by whether the ovum has been fertilized by sperm. Among bees and ants, for example, unfertilized eggs produce males, and fertilized ones, females. Individuals conceived *parthenogenetically*, that is, without the fertilization of the ovum by sperm, occur spontaneously in many species and have also been produced

7 Age and Sex in Evolutionary Perspective

under artificial laboratory stimulation in vertebrates and even mammals. Parthenogenetic rabbit embryos, for example, have been induced, although they have not yet proved viable. It is not inconceivable that they might one day prove so. In mammals, parthenogenesis produces only females. Normally, however, vertebrates and more specifically mammals reproduce through the intervention of *haploid gametes* produced by animals of both sexes, which combine to produce viable *diploid* individuals.[1]

There is one aspect of sexual differentiation, however, that varies greatly and in no discernible evolutionary direction among vertebrate species, namely sexual *dimorphism*. This term means the degree to which males and females of the same species differ from each other in their *secondary sexual characteristics*, that is, in their physical appearance other than their reproductive organs. In some species, male and female are almost indistinguishable in size and appearance; in others the differences are striking. Among many fishes, birds, and reptiles, for example, there are great differences in the coloration of the epidermis or the plumage; the male is generally (but not always) brighter and the female drabber. From the point of view of sexual dominance, the most important aspect of dimorphism is probably the relative size of males and females. Here, too, the range of dimorphism is enormous. In most species, the male is bigger than the female, being sometimes over twice her weight, and sometimes just slightly larger. In a few species, however, males and females have appreciably the same mean size, and occasionally, as with some spiders, the female is several times the size of the male.

Sexual dimorphism, especially differences in relative size, seems to correlate with the relative dominance of the sexes. Among some spiders, it takes a fleet-legged male to avoid being cannibalized by his mate immediately after copulation. Among the "social" insects, among which reproduction is left to a few oversized fertile females that spend their lifetime laying eggs (for example, bees, ants, and termites), the role of males is largely limited to defense against competing species or, indeed, almost totally parasitic (for example, drone bees). On the other hand, when the male is clearly

---

[1] In complex organisms, a distinction is made between the *somatic* or body cells which make up the organism and the *gametes* or reproductive cells produced by the ovaries and testes. The former are *diploid*, that is, they normally have the full complement of chromosomes characteristic of the species, while the latter are *haploid*, or have half that number. The complex cellular process through which a diploid cell splits into two haploid cells is known as *meiosis*. On conception, the two haploid gametes fuse into a new diploid organism.

bigger than the female, as with many mammals, male dominance is often evident. Among many bird species in which sexual dimorphism takes more the form of brilliance of plumage than of size differences, there seems to be a great degree of sexual equality and sharing of nurturance tasks for the young.

The second evolutionary trend that we noted concerned the relationship between the degree of development of the organism and what, for lack of a better term, we might call the physical proximity of the sex act. It is true that insects, arachnids, crustaceans, and other invertebrates reproduce themselves through an act of copulation, if by that is meant direct contact between the sexual organs of the male and female. From the hominid perspective, the invertebrates, however, can be regarded as altogether different lines of evolution, some of them highly developed and successful in their own right, but of limited relevance to our own biology. Looking at the vertebrates, the trend toward greater physical proximity is clear. In most fishes, the male ejaculates sperm over the eggs after they have been laid by the female, notwithstanding a few viviparous (producing live young instead of eggs) species. Amphibians, reptiles, and birds normally must come into direct physical contact to reproduce, but very few achieve the degree of interpenetration of sexual organs achieved by mammals.

This growing "closeness" in the sexual act has great significance for reproductive economy and efficiency. Sexuality is an adaptive mechanism whereby the probability of fertilization of any given ovum increases along the evolutionary scale. In the higher organisms, combined with decreases in both fecundity and infant mortality, the reproductive process becomes increasingly parsimonious. Yet, equally important, this economy is accomplished without loss of genetic variation. As the ratio of sperm to ova remains on the order of millions to one even among the most developed mammals, the possible range of genetic diversity derived from a single egg thus remains enormous.

Degree and length of dependence of infants on adults are also closely related to evolutionary development among vertebrates. Some insects spend most of their life cycle in nonadult forms, but the dependence of the subadult on the adult is typically minimal (except among the social insects). Here again, the invertebrates can be regarded as outside the evolutionary line that gave rise to our species and are thus of limited relevance to us. Many of the fishes and reptiles take a long time to grow to their adult size, and some keep growing for most of their lives, but the dependence of the young on the adult is not only minimal but frequently reversed. The propensity of many fish species to cannibalize their young with the greatest gusto is well known to keepers of aquaria. Some lizards are not adverse to eating their own eggs. Amphibians

9 Age and Sex in Evolutionary Perspective

have the characteristic, like insects, of undergoing a profound metamorphosis between their infant and adult stage, but the dependence of tadpoles on adults is nil.

Birds, as warm-blooded animals, represent a clear evolutionary change. The relative thermal homeostasis of their internal environment partially emancipates them, like mammals, from the effects of temperature fluctuations in their external environment. Their young mature quickly, but until they are capable of flying, most of them go through a phase of utter dependence on adults for food. Among mammals, lactation is a further giant step in the direction of dependence of infants on adults, and, unlike among birds, on *female* adults. For birds, nurturance is an onus frequently shared equally by the adults of both sexes. Lactation represents another abrupt transition in the evolutionary process of sex differentiation.

All mammals suckle their young (barring artificial feeding in *Homo sapiens*, who sometimes become dependent on the female of another species to permit the emancipation of its own females from the chore), but, among mammalian species, there are vast differences in the length of gestation, lactation, and maturation, both in absolute duration, and relative to the life span of the organism. Gestation ranges from a few weeks to between one and two years, generally increasing in time with the size of the mammal. Primates have among the longest gestation periods, but so do other large mammals such as bovines, equines, and pachyderms. Maturation to adult size ranges from a few weeks to a decade or more, the latter limit being shared by *Homo sapiens*, the great apes, and the two species of elephants. These few species spend approximately one-fourth of their normal life span growing up, compared to one-tenth for a dog and even less for most rodents. The degree of helplessness of infants at birth varies greatly, being total for man, the great apes, and many carnivores and rodents, and much less for herbivores. The great dependence and clinging to their mothers of primate infants is part of man's biological heritage (Bowlby, 1969). The period of dependence is longest for man, but the apes and the elephants are not far behind, lactation lasting approximately one to two years.

Fecundity is negatively correlated with vertebrate evolution. Fish typically lay thousands of eggs at a time; amphibians hundreds; and reptiles scores. Mammals and birds seldom give birth to more than a dozen young at a time, and many species bear less than half a dozen. By and large, size among mammals is inversely correlated with fecundity. Most rodents have four to eight young, whereas large herbivores, whales, elephants, and rhinoceroses typically have single or twin births. Considering their size, the larger carnivores are relatively prolific, and the primates, with their single birth pattern, unprolific.

Infant mortality and fecundity tend to decrease in parallel fashion up the evolutionary scale. For example, the historical rate of 50 percent mortality for human infants, which may still exist in some parts of the world, may seem high by modern standards, but is in fact quite low in comparison with most nonmammalian species. Among the highly prolific fish, the vast majority of the young are gobbled up as links somewhere along the food chain. Among the unprolific herbivores, predators take their toll mostly from the lame and senile rather than from the young, speed being the main defense of herbivores. Most primate species defend themselves adequately from predators either through arboreal mobility or, among the terrestrial species, through collectively organized protection. Other large and unprolific mammals such as whales, rhinoceroses, and elephants are protected by their bulk: few if any predators are big enough to tackle them.

Finally, there is a general relationship between vertebrate evolution and longevity. Although a few reptiles, such as some species of turtles and crocodiles, have a life span that approaches or even exceeds that of the primates, the more developed animals tend to live longer, and so do the larger ones. Among the mammals, apes and elephants approach man's in their life span. Most large mammals tend to live from ten to twenty years; the smaller ones typically live from three to ten years. It is noteworthy that only a few mammalian species, man included, can experience genuine senility. Most animals fall prey to predators, or if they are carnivores they become unable to hunt their quarry before they attain senility. Elephants, which are herbivorous and without natural enemies, can grow senile; so can some terrestrial primates, because of their protective social organization.

We have, if only cursorily, surveyed some of the characteristics of age and sex differentiation in a phylogenetic or evolutionary perspective. *Homo sapiens*, as one biological species among millions, shares a long evolutionary history with other animals. The longer is the common evolutionary road travelled by our species and others, the closer are the biological similarities between them, and thus, the more we can learn by comparing our biology with theirs. A general survey of mammals would take us too far afield, even though some distantly related mammals, such as the elephant, show odd resemblances to humans in life span, maturation, gestation, and fecundity. Our fellow primates, however, from whom we have diverged in our evolution for a mere two or three million years, share a good deal in common with us, and deserve a much closer look. Particularly relevant to our study are the Old World monkeys and the great apes. The next chapter proposes to show that man is indeed very much a primate, only more so.

2 Age and Sex among Primates

In the last decade, scientists have made a number of carefully documented observational and experimental studies concerning the behavior of many primate species in zoos, in the wild, and under semiwild conditions. Anthropologists have long been aware of the relevance of primatology to their discipline; but sociologists who, for the most part, have yet to incorporate into their frame of reference the findings from non-Western human societies, are even more reluctant to look beyond their own species.

Primate studies are doubly relevant to our understanding of man. First, the comparison of different species, to the extent that it reveals similarities, helps us define the biologically determined parameters of human behavior. Second, variations in behavior *within* a species, for example under zoo contrasted with wild conditions, give us an idea of the extent of environmental determination of behavior in subhumans. Given the until recently dominant biases of the social sciences that, for all intents and purposes, the behavior of man is learned and that of "lower animals" is genetically inherited, a closer look at the primates is bound to be instructive.

However, we must exercise caution in applying evidence from primates to an interpretation of human evolution. The temptation is strong to treat monkeys and apes as the next best thing we have to extinct hominid forms, and thus to infer the origins of man from the behavior of contemporary primates. A similar fallacy was perpetrated in early anthropology by treating contemporary "primitive" societies as surviving ancestral forms of contemporary "advanced" societies. This was a fallacy of unilinear evolutionism. Twentieth-century rain forest pygmy hunters are no more living ancestors of Tokyo insurance brokers, Paris bakers, or Lagos physicians, than living chimpanzees are protomen stopped dead in their evolutionary tracks. In the case of both biological and social evolution, different contemporary species and societies represent *different lines of evolution* and adaptation to specific environments. Thus, we are not interested in monkeys and apes as men arrested in their development, which they clearly are not, but as fellow primates who share with us a basic biological heritage.

The primates include 189 living species, 166 of them arboreal, and not all of equal relevance to man (Napier, 1970, p. 68). The lower primates, including lemurs, tree shrews, tarsiers, bushbabies, and other families are mostly nocturnal and arboreal, and are too distantly related to man to be of direct interest. Of the higher primates or *Anthropoidea*, the many species of New World monkeys, characterized by their prehensile tails and generally arboreal habits, and including howlers, capuchins, squirrel monkeys, spider monkeys, marmosets, tamarins, and others are more distantly related to man than the Old World monkeys (*Cercopithecidae*) and the apes (*Pongidae*), which shall primarily concern us here. The *Cercopithecidae* include nearly sixty species, both arboreal and terrestrial, including macaques, baboons, mandrills, guenons, and langurs. The *Pongidae* or apes include seven species of gibbons, two of chimpanzees, and the orangutan and gorilla. Together with the one surviving species of *Hominidae*, they form with us the superfamily of *Hominoidea*. So much for our family tree.[1]

Zuckerman's pioneer study (1932) of hamadryas baboons (*Papio hamadryas*) at the London Zoo created for a long time a commonly accepted stereotype of primate societies. To be sure, in their propensity toward male domination, the hamadryas baboons are quite human, and it is difficult to resist the temptation to anthropomorphize when describing their social structure, as we shall see later. Primate societies were long held to be under the domination of an adult male surrounded by a harem of submissive females over whom he maintained a monopoly of sexual access. Juveniles and females with infants were treated somewhat more permissively, but other adult males were excluded from the group and from access to females until one of them became strong enough to displace the ruling despot. Even for hamadryas baboons, this picture is an oversimplification, and studies of other primate species in the wild did not replicate some of the earlier zoo studies. Other closely related baboon species, for example, showed that females in heat copulated quite freely with a variety of males, though temporarily tending to pair off with one male during the peak of a given oestrus.

---

[1] For a good tabular presentation of the taxonomy of primates, see Ramona and Desmond Morris, *Men and Apes* (1966, p. 167).

13 Age and Sex among Primates

A first hypothesis was that zoos were an unnatural environment in which to observe primates, and hence that their behavior under such conditions was a poor predictor of their behavior in the wild. One ingenious theory was that since the food supply in a zoo is regular and abundant, animals do not need to compete much for it. On the other hand, since sex is the main distraction for animals in captivity, it acquires great importance and is competed for among males. In a simian analog to the Noble Savage theory, monkeys were held to be as corrupted by civilization as men, hence the need to observe them in the wild where presumably their behavior, uncontaminated by human perversions, would exhibit its authentic nature.

No doubt, field studies of primate societies are superior to zoo studies, because zoos do impose severe constraints on animal behavior. An orangutan in a cement-floored cage, for example, is hardly in a position to demonstrate how arboreal a creature he is; and a male hamadryas baboon with a single mate is hard put to give vent to his polygynous proclivities. Notwithstanding the limitations of zoos, three interesting general conclusions can be drawn from both field and zoo studies of primates. First, to the extent that zoo conditions permit primates to engage in a certain type of behavior that is natural to them, they will tend to do so. In other words, primates exhibit some intraspecific uniformities in behavior and social organization, unless certain forms of behavior are obviously blocked by limitations in the physical environment. Wild hamadryas baboons, for example, behave much as they do in zoos that have a large enough colony of them and the appropriate sex ratio to enable them to reproduce a society on the hamadryas scale. Research findings thus tend to confirm the importance of genetic predispositions in primate behavior.

Second, zoo and wild studies of primates have shown an extremely wide range of behavioral characteristics from species to species, even between closely related ones. It appears much less risky to extrapolate from zoo to wild behavior within a given species, than to generalize from one species to another. Not all monkeys are alike.

Third, compared to less intelligent mammals, primates exhibit a greater ability to learn from experience and to modify their behavior and social organization to adapt to environmental changes.[2] Despite the fact that each species seems to have a

---

[2]Crook and Gartlan (1966) make a useful taxonomic attempt at sorting out the effect of ecology on primate social organization. Much of the ecological adaptation of a given species, such as sexual dimorphism, is genetically transmitted rather than learned, but some aspects of social organization, such as size of the group, can vary widely within the same species

genetic "blueprint" that broadly determines parameters of behavior, different groups of the same species have been reported to have different social organizations, group sizes, or leadership patterns, possibly in response to ecological pressures, or to adapt their individual and collective behavior in response to changes introduced by man (Kawamura, 1963; Frisch, 1968; Gartlan, 1968; Yoshiba, 1968; Denham, 1970; Mason, 1971; Miller, 1971). There is even evidence of transmission of learned behavior through social communication, a characteristic of culture that was once thought a human monopoly (Miller, 1971). This is true not only of our close relatives, the apes, but also of our more distant cousins, the monkeys.

Of all primates, the great apes are most relevant to man by virtue of our close phylogenetic relationship. Next to these, however, the terrestrial *Cercopithecidae*, especially the baboons, seem most worthy of our attention, if only because of the scale and complexity of their social organization and the basic similarity of habitat, diet, and modes of food gathering to the direct hominid ancestors of *Homo sapiens*.

Turning first to the great apes, we know least about the orangutan. In the wild, the animal is rare and elusive. Richard Davenport, who undertook the most extensive field study of orangs, encountered only sixteen animals in seven months. Few zoos have any adult orangs, much less enough of them to report on their social behavior. (Young orangs are usually captured by killing the mother, thereby threatening the survival of the species.) The little we do know about orangs makes them the most implausible of primates. Despite their bulk, they are arboreal, but unlike gibbons who swing from branch to branch (*brachiate*) with great agility and speed, orangs move slowly and clumsily, managing a bare three miles an hour in tree tops, the speed of a man's walk (Reynolds, 1967, p. 157). The orangutan also appears to be the least sociable of primates. Of the sixteen orangs Davenport sighted, three were in a group consisting of an adult male, an adult female, and an infant; on three occasions he located a mother and infant; the other seven animals (four adults, three adolescents) were entirely alone (*ibid.*, p. 158). Sexual dimorphism is pronounced among orangs, males weighing twice as much as females (Table 1), but there are no observational data on male dominance. In zoos, young orangs are playful and interact freely with other young apes if put in the same cage, but adult orangs are remarkably inactive.

---

depending on environmental factors (Kummer, 1968). Certainly, the old heredity-environment controversy is based on a false dichotomy since so much of the environmental adaptation becomes genetically transmitted through natural selection.

TABLE 1

Mean Weight of Females in Percent of Mean Weight of Males among Pongidae Species

	Average Female Weight in Percent of Average Male Weight
Gibbon (*Hylobates lar*)	93
Gibbon (*Hylobates concolor*)	103
Gibbon (*Hylobates hoolock*)	96
Gibbon (*Hylobates klossii*)	105
Siamang	92
Orangutan	49
Chimpanzee	88
Gorilla	48
Man	89

(Adapted from Schultz, 1969.)

Gibbons, represented by seven closely related species, are far more numerous and successfully adapted to their surroundings than orangutans. Observed in the wild by C. Ray Carpenter (1946), John Ellefson (1968), and others, and common in zoos, their habits are far better known. Perhaps the two most striking behavioral characteristics of gibbons, frequently observed in zoos, are their extraordinarily agile brachiation splendidly adapted to their entirely arboreal existence, and their strident vocalizations. The gibbon species best observed in the wild, *Hylobates lar*, was found to have much the same kind of social organization in both areas of observation, Thailand and Malaysia. If the reader will pardon the anthropomorphism, gibbons have what sociologists call monogamous, neolocal, nuclear families that typically consist of four animals: the adult couple, one juvenile, and one infant. Gibbons, at least of that species, are highly territorial. Each family forages fruit, leaves, buds, and flowers in a well-defined area ranging from 30 to 300 acres, and scares off its neighbors by vocal displays and shaking branches. Families sleep in trees in the middle of their territory. Though the process has not been observed, it seems that juveniles, on reaching sexual maturity, pair off and establish a separate new family. The fact that young adult males were observed to be repulsed by older paired males, and the absence of family groups with several adult females would lead one to that conclusion. This would imply the absence of inbreeding within the nuclear family, and would also raise the question of how uniquely human the incest taboo is (Aberle et al., 1963). Observers of gibbons have not seen any evidence of male dominance, a feature probably associated with the nearly complete absence of sexual dimorphism in gibbons. In body weight, male and female gibbons average well under 10 percent difference, and, in some species, females may even be slightly larger than males (Table 1). Sexual behavior seems uncommon. Carpenter, for example, observed only two copulations in the course of his field work (Reynolds, 1967, pp. 152-55).

About the other great ape species, we know a great deal. There are thousands of chimpanzees in captivity and their occupations have ranged from film star, experimental subject, and circus performer to cosmonaut. Gorillas are much scarcer, especially adults, but every major zoo has one or more. Both animals have been systematically observed in the wild during the last fifteen years (Kawai & Mizuhara, 1959; Schaller, 1963; van Lawick-Goodall, 1969). Both animals are native to the African rain forest and are partly arboreal and partly terrestrial. The maturation period of about a decade is much the same for chimpanzees and gorillas, as are the gestation period and the degree of infant dependency. Among chimpanzees, however, sexual dimorphism is moderate, much as in *Homo sapiens*, while among gorillas it is pronounced (Table 1).

There are appreciable differences in social structure between chimpanzees and gorillas. Using anthropomorphic terminology, Kawai and Mizuhara (1959, p. 18) state, "a gorilla troop consists of one adult male as leader, young males, and females and infants; that is, a troop of gorillas seems to be one polygamous family." The four troops they observed ranged in size from five to eighteen animals, but even the larger troops had only one adult male; the number of adult or near adult females ranged from two to four. The young males were peripheral to the troop, and Kawai and Mizuhara (1959, pp. 35-36) theorize that when young males reach adulthood, they come in conflict with the troop leader and father, and either become solitary or manage to take a young female with them and establish a new family. Again, the authors anthropomorphize and talk of a mother-son incest prohibition. Schaller's (1963) observations do not support the polygamous family view of gorilla troops, for although one male is clearly the leader of the troop, larger troops have more than one silver-backed (fully grown) male, and the leader does not seek to maintain a sexual monopoly over females. His leadership is expressed in directing the troop's movements and protecting its retreat from intruders. Kawai and Mizuhara speculate that ties between animals and separation between troops are determined by kinship and sexual relationship to the troop leader (in the case of the females). Gorilla troops do not defend a given territory, and the areas foraged by various troops overlap.

Despite his undeserved reputation for ferocity, the gorilla is a peace loving animal, and, unlike the chimpanzee, who has been observed eating meat, a strict vegetarian. When threatened, as by a human presence, male gorillas make impressive displays to frighten off intruders, including noisy chest-beating with cupped hands, and mock charges that stop short of physical contact if the intruder stands his ground.

The most extensive account of gorilla behavior and ecology is given by Schaller (1963), whose observations confirm or complement those of other scholars. Schaller observed well-differentiated age classes: newborn babies are completely helpless for the first two or three months; by the age of four months, they begin to adopt quadrupedal locomotion and become mobile, but are still dependent infants; after two or three years, infants become independent juveniles; by age eight to ten, gorillas become adult, but, among males, a further differentiation exists between the young black-backed male and the fully grown silver-backed male. The latter *age grade* goes together with troop leadership. Schaller observed troops as large as twenty-seven individuals and confirms both the stability of the social group and its male leadership pattern.

Schaller reports detailed information on dominance behavior, which he observed 110 times, but which occupied a relatively minor share of total gorilla behavior. Fighting and other forms of aggression are quite exceptional; instead, dominance is expressed mostly through staring or a light tap on the back, and submission by crouching and yielding one's place. Dominance order is based on both age and sex. The silver-backed males outrank all others, and among silver-backed males, those in the prime of life outrank both the younger and the older ones. There is no clear order of dominance as between adult females and black-backed males (when the sexual dimorphism is not yet as pronounced as with silver-backed males). Females with small infants tend to dominate both females without infants and those with older infants. Adults of both sexes dominate all subadults. Among subadults, dominance is a function of size and hence of age, juveniles outranking infants. The interesting feature of the gorilla dominance order is that, while it is quite unambiguously established, it is not very salient compared to other forms of behavior, and it is gently enforced.

Gorillas, though living in well-defined and stable social groups, are not very sociable. Grooming, for example, which is a time-consuming and extremely significant form of interaction among many primates, is infrequent among adult gorillas, but females groom infants and adults groom themselves. Grooming thus seems to be mainly a utilitarian rather than a social activity for gorillas (Schaller, 1963, p. 248). Infants and juveniles play together, but less intensively than the young of many other primate species. Black-backed males stay out of reach of the dominant silver-backed ones, and the latter largely ignore the former. Sexual activity is rare. Schaller observed only two copulations in the field. From zoo observations, however, we know that gorillas, though hardly living up to their oversexed reputation of Hollywood jungle movies, display quasihuman imagination in copulatory positions when the fancy strikes them. Receptive females initiate sexual behavior by presenting their genitalia to males and fondling and licking the male's testes. The dominant male in a troop does not seem to enforce a sexual monopoly over females; in both copulatory acts witnessed by Schaller, a female was mounted by a silver-backed but nondominant male without much interference, much less aggression, from the troop leader. On one occasion, the leader slowly approached the couple, who temporarily separated, but later resumed intercourse when the indifferent leader was fifteen feet away (Schaller, 1963, pp. 282-84).

A general picture of gorilla "national character" clearly emerges from both zoo and field observations. Gorillas are peace loving, introverted animals, living in stable social groups dominated by a male in his prime. All forms of interaction between adults, however, are relatively rare, including aggression, grooming, and sexual activity, so common among other primates. Gorilla society seems to be of the easy-going, live-and-let-live type; male and adult dominance, though clear, are gently and even negligently enforced, despite great sexual dimorphism.

Chimpanzee behavior, as observed in the wild by Adriaan Kortlandt (1962), Vernon Reynolds (1967), Jane van Lawick-Goodall (1965, 1968), and others is also fairly well known. Of the studies, the field work of Jane van Lawick-Goodall is justly famous, if only because she achieved a degree of empathy with her apes that few anthropologists develop with their human subjects. And, indeed, from her suspiciously pro-chimp accounts, chimpanzee society comes out amazingly close to the communal utopias dreamed of by contemporary visionaries. Goodall might argue, I suppose, that chimpanzees easily achieve what men only dream of because they are more agreeable and likeable fellows to start with. Be that as it may, chimpanzees seem to have achieved a peaceful, noncompetitive, noncoercive, nonpossessive, nontyrannical kind of society. The most manlike of primates through their physiological and anatomical makeup, through their documented use of tools in the wild, and through their complex vocalizations and communication systems, chimpanzees are among the least manlike in their social lives.

Compared to gorillas, chimps live in larger but more unstable groups; they are less hierarchical and more sociable.

19 Age and Sex among Primates

Like gorillas, chimps are nonterritorial. Groups which may be as large as fifty are frequently changing in composition and have overlapping foraging ranges. There is no defense of the range and little hostility among groups, except for threat displays among males. Chimps, smaller and more agile than gorillas, are more arboreal and they brachiate. On the ground, both apes use their unique quadrupedal "knuckle walking," leaning on the middle phalanxes of the folded fingers of their forelimbs. Both occasionally use bipedal locomotion for short distances, and "knuckle walking" has been speculated to be a transitional stage to bipedalism. Chimps, though predominantly vegetarian, are more omnivorous than gorillas; they eat insects, and occasionally kill and eat small mammals, such as monkeys, small antelopes, and young bush pigs.

An essential feature of chimpanzee social organization is that they form two functionally distinct types of groups, as first noted by Kortlandt (1962). There are what he called "nursery groups" made up of females with dependent infants, and "sexual groups" composed of adults and juveniles of both sexes. Sexual groups tend to be far noisier, more mobile, and larger than nursery groups. Both types of groups, however, are open and hence unstable—individuals are free to join and leave their groups as the fancy strikes them (van Lawick-Goodall, 1965, 1968; Reynolds, 1967). Although adults have a dominance order, and males from different groups do engage in threat displays to establish a dominance order among them, chimp groups have no well-defined leaders.

Chimps are quite gregarious and sociable. Goodall (1965, 1968) established that they greet each other by touching each other's head, shoulder, or genitalia; that they seem to recognize ties of friendship or kinship even after periods of spatial separation; that they share and solicit food by extending a hand palm upmost; that they show sibling rivalry and jealousy, and other such human emotions; that young chimps use objects as toys; that they use sticks and leaves as tools; and that they communicate with each other through more than twenty types of vocalization. Chimps also engage in extensive grooming among adults, sessions lasting up to two hours and involving sometimes half a dozen individuals. They also participate in forms of collective behavior (such as stamping the ground, waving branches, and vocalizing in unison), which one has difficulty in resisting the temptation of calling "ritualistic."

Mother-infant ties extensively documented by Goodall are very strong, and infant dependence is great and prolonged. The infant chimp is kept within two feet of the mother for the first six months. Until that time, the infant clings to its mother's belly; between six and eighteen months, infants ride on their mother's back. Suckling lasts two to three years, long after infants have begun eating solid foods. Mother-child ties continue to persist into adolescence and perhaps even into adulthood.

If the nurturance relationship is potent, chimps do not show any trace of what might be termed a "marital" tie. Chimps are much less sexually inhibited than gorillas. The genitalia of females in oestrus swell to the size of a baseball. Females are quite promiscuous: Goodall observed one female copulating with seven males in rapid succession. Sometimes the female solicits copulation by crouching and presenting her genitalia to the male; sometimes the male attracts the female through a "courtship display." Sexual jealousy and attempts by dominant males to restrict access to females are totally absent, and there is nothing approaching stable pairs. In captivity, chimps are inventive in their sex play and copulatory positions, and casual zoo visitors are frequently treated to a display worthy of a simian *Kama Sutra*. This might be an elaboration grown out of the boredom of life in cages. In the wild, chimp imagination seems less narrowly channelled. Both in the wild and in captivity, however, chimps copulate without making much fuss over it. Relations between the sexes appear relatively egalitarian.

Although, in respect to their intelligence and emotions, chimpanzees are the most human of primates, they are more than humanly gentle and tolerant of each other. The hierarchical social order of some of our more distantly related terrestrial cousins, the baboons, gives us a much better reflection of human societies. Terrestrial monkeys, living for the most part in semiarid open plains, lack the cover and protection from predators enjoyed by the arboreal species. They protect themselves through the safety of organized numbers. Sexual dimorphism is typically pronounced, males weighing twice to 2-1/2 times as much as females, and groups of males provide collective defense. Baboon societies tend to be hierarchical, disciplined, aggressive, and male dominated, much like their human counterparts. In arboreal species, conversely, the necessity of escaping predators through flight in trees reduces the adaptive value of size dimorphism, and hence the protective function of males.

The social behavior of baboons, macaques, and other gregarious species of monkeys has long been observed in zoos (Zuckerman, 1932) and in semiwild conditions (Southwick, 1963; De Vore, 1965). Most large zoos have a "monkey island" in which a substantial colony of *Cercopithecidae* (usually a baboon or macaque species) can readily be studied. In more recent years, these observations have been supplemented by a number of excellent field studies, especially of baboons (Washburn & De Vore, 1961*a* and *b*; De Vore, 1962; De Vore & Washburn, 1963; Kummer, 1968; Altmann, 1970). Since they live mostly in open savannah country, observing baboons in the wild is relatively easy, especially in the East African game reserves where animals have become quite tame. The main difficulty of such studies is the sheer size of these societies: there is too much to see, observe, and record. This is a far cry from tracking elusive apes in dense rain forests.

Two species of baboons are among the best known—*Papio hamadryas* and the so-called savannah baboons (*Papio anubis*, *Papio cynocephalus*, and *Papio ursinus*). Although they are closely related genetically, they are quite differently organized socially. The savannah baboons are all organized in foraging bands that vary in size from a dozen to some 200 individuals, and average between 40 and 50. These bands are strongly dominated by an oligarchy of adult males who fight off subordinate and subadult males and share females in oestrus. The females of the band thus constitute a kind of vast collective pool, and mate promiscuously with any of the dominant males or indeed even with juvenile and nondominant males before they attain the peak of their sexual receptivity (Morris, 1966, pp. 175-76).

Another well-studied species, *Macaca fuscata*, observed for two decades at the Japanese Monkey Center by Junichiro Itani and others, exhibits a social organization similar to that of baboons, except that the oligarchy of dominant males, itself internally hierarchized with a supreme ruler, attempts to exclude subordinate males from access to females. Subordinate males stay on the periphery of the group and are fought off by the leaders when they try to gain access to females in oestrus (Morris, 1966, pp. 173-74). When a female is in heat, she develops a brief consort relationship with one of the dominant males for a period of two or three days. Among rhesus monkeys observed by Carpenter, females mate more promiscuously with several or all of the dominant males in their group (Morris, 1966, pp. 174-75).

The hamadryas baboon differs markedly in his social organization from the savannah baboons and the macaques just described. Studied in the London Zoo by Zuckerman (1932) forty years ago, and recently in the field by Kummer (1968) and Kurt, the hamadryas baboon exposed an interesting series of errors among primatologists. Zuckerman's pioneer study had led others to assume that the "harem" pattern found among captive hamadryas baboons was common to all baboons, and indeed was the prototype of primate social organization. When field studies of macaques and other baboons did not show any harems, it was widely assumed that the dominant and possessive behavior of hamadryas males reported by Zuckerman was a perversion brought about by zoo conditions. What might be termed the "nothing-else-to-do" theory postulated that in captivity, where food was plentiful, males would fight over and try to monopolize females as the most desirable resource. In the wild, it was thought, where sex was plentiful and food more problematic, the priorities would be reversed. The argument was conclusively invalidated by Kummer's masterly study (1968) of *Papio hamadryas* in Ethiopia. He found that wild hamadryas baboons had harems also and behaved much as did their fellow species members in captivity. Hamadryas baboons are simply different from most other baboons and macaques, and primate behavior, though greatly modifiable through environmental changes, also seems partly determined in many respects by genetically transmitted predispositions.

Kummer's monograph is probably the most informative single study of age and sex differentiation and social structure in a primate species. In fact, it reads almost like an anthropological monograph. In some respects, hamadryas society is so much like human societies that it deserves close examination. Unlike what has been misnamed polygyny in gorillas and other primates, the hamadryas are truly polygynous, and the temptation to anthropomorphize their social structure is strong. Kummer observed 23 samples including 2,770 animals living in the semiarid environment of Eastern Ethiopia. The hamadryas are organized at three distinct levels, which Kummer calls, respectively, the one-male unit, the band, and the troop. Troops average about 120 individuals, but some are as large as 750 or as small as 12. The troop might be described as a "dormitory community." It consists of those baboons who share a steep, rocky ledge to sleep at night, protected from predators. Membership in a given troop fluctuates, and the size of the troop is determined by the availability of suitable rocks: where rocks are scarce, troops are large; where plentiful, troops are small. The troop, then, seems to be an ecological adaptation that is not genetically determined (Kummer, 1968, p. 148). Hamadryas have a capacity for "fission and fusion" in the social groupings in response to changing environmental conditions (*ibid.*, p. 155).

Each morning after waking up, the troop leaves its ledge and congregates above it on flat ground. This is a time for sociability, most notably for grooming and copulation. After a while, the troop breaks up into bands, in effect foraging parties, which spend the remainder of the day together roaming over the parched semidesert and feeding. Hamadryas, like other baboons, are occasionally carnivorous, and they dig for water when surface water is unavailable. The band, ranging in size from thirty to ninety, is stabler in composition than the troop. This level of social organization of the hamadryas—the band—has its closest counterpart in other baboon and macaque species.

Unlike in other species, however, the hamadryas band is subdivided into one-male units, and as an elaboration thereof, two-male units. These one-male units are relatively stable and constitute, in effect, polygynous families. One adult male in his prime exercises control over several adult females, their offspring, and one or more subadult male "followers." In Kummer's words (p. 150):

> ... hamadryas society is an exclusive society of males, the females being distributed among its members as controlled dependents who have no active part in the life of the higher units. Consequently, the hamadryas organization is based on two types of social bonds: the bond between the adult male and his female, and the bond among the adult males.

The polygynous family is held together by the sheer force of its leader. The leader keeps his females, whether in oestrus or not, within close physical proximity of him, under penalty of a graduated series of threats ranging from raised brows and lunging to a bite in the shoulder or back. The females avoid punishment by staying mostly within three to four yards of the unit leader, or, after a transgression, by running back, crouching motionless, or "presenting" their genitalia to the leader. Leaders never copulate with females other than their own (who average 2.3 per one-male unit, but may be as many as 7), but females do "present" and mate with subadult male followers behind the leader's back. Females are usually punished by a bite when caught, and transgressing females in oestrus are often seen running to the leader and "presenting" to him in atonement for an unnoticed clandestine affair with a juvenile male. Adult males without females, who stay on the periphery of the band and are beaten back from access to females, "may remain without copulating for years" (Kummer, p. 41). It is noteworthy that the aggressive herding behavior of the leader applies to females in and out of oestrus. Male dominance is not only a means of sexual monopolization (which is only partly successful with juvenile males), but, first and foremost, the basis of the unit's cohesion (*ibid.*, p. 39). Leaders force females to follow and surround them, whether females are sexually receptive or not.

The one-male unit sometimes takes a more complex form through the association of two unit leaders. As leaders become older, their interest in females and their despotic control over them decreases, but their influence in the band increases, especially in determining the direction of movement during foraging. At the same time, they lose some females, the harem typically dwindling to one or at most two females. A number of composite units are brought into existence through the association of a male in his prime with a harem of three or more females, and an older male with one or two females of his own whose main leadership activity is directed toward the larger band.

Kummer suggests an explanation for this three-level social organization of hamadryas baboons, compared to the far simpler one-level band organization of savannah baboons. Band organization is a protective system against predators such as leopards and cheetahs. The hamadryas live in a more arid environment where food is scarcer, and where tree groves on which to perch at night to escape predators are almost nonexistent. The smaller one-male units are a response to the need to scatter more widely in search of food; the large troops are a result of the scarcity of safe night quarters.

The two salient principles of role differentiation in hamadryas society are clearly age and sex. Females bear and nurture the young; males provide protection and coordination of movements in the larger units. Different phases of the life cycle, marked by clear changes in size and hair color, are accompanied by radical alterations in behavior. The newborn black infants are highly dependent until four to six months of age and are treated with interest and tolerance by all older animals. When the infant loses his black coat and becomes brown, he is expected to become more independent. Weaning takes place around one year, and tolerance of adult males toward year-old infants diminishes. By the age of eighteen months, juveniles begin to leave their mothers and group by sex. The females now approaching nubility begin to be taken over by an adult male; the males begin to congregate in peripheral groups of male age peers. Some females begin to show oestral swellings at age two, but they seem to become fertile only around age four. The fully grown male develops a mantle of brown hair that becomes silver-colored as he ages. Here, too, the role differentiation between the younger polygynous unit leaders in their prime and the older band leaders is, to some degree, marked by age polymorphism, that is, by visible changes in physical appearance associated with age. Subadult males are permitted some degree of sexual and grooming activity with subadult or even adult females without eliciting the punitive reaction of the unit leader that an adult male would. Older males become less aggressive toward the females and allow them greater freedom of movement. Adult males are more tolerant of, and less interested in, subadult than in adult females. Aggression, submission, grooming, copulation, and other forms of behavior are clearly differentiated by age and sex.

Another very human feature of hamadryas baboons is that their aggressiveness is not limited to other species or to individuals within their groups, as is the case with most primates. Hamadryas bands fight against other bands when their component units get spatially intermingled (Kummer, p. 149). Bands are held together, Kummer demonstrated experimentally, by the fact that the male unit leaders within the band inhibit themselves and each other from competing for their respective females. This is achieved by each unit leader's herding his females around him, and by keeping his distance from his fellow unit leaders and their females. The inhibition breaks down if spatial intermingling occurs, and if intermingling occurs between bands that are strangers to one another, generalized group fighting can break out. Kummer experimentally transplanted two one-male units into unfamiliar troops: one unit managed to escape from the troop; the other was attacked and its females were taken over by unit leaders of the troop.

To summarize, what does our excursion into the social world of primates suggest for our own species? First, we must repeat our initial caution: monkeys and apes are collateral relatives of ours, not ancestors. Their behavior and social organization represent synchronous but quite distinct lines of evolution, which do not permit us to make simple sequential inferences running from monkeys, to apes, to men. This should be obvious from the lack of any clear relationship between phylogenetic closeness and the similarity of social organization. For example, the hamadryas baboon, a distant relative of man, has the most complex and most humanlike primate social organization on record. On the other hand, the great apes, much closer cousins of ours, are very unlike us in their collective behavior: orangutans seem to have almost no collective behavior except for the mother-infant tie and fleeting sexual encounters; gibbons have monogamous families; chimpanzees have peaceful, egalitarian, noncompetitive, promiscuous communes such as only the most idealistic humans attempt to create, and not very successfully at that.

Likewise, in an important morphological aspect of male-female relationships, namely sexual dimorphism, there is no clear evolutionary trend. Two great apes, gorillas and orangs, are highly dimorphic; the chimp, like us, is only moderately so; the gibbon hardly at all. Among monkeys, baboons are highly dimorphic whereas, in other species, males and females are hardly distinguishable. For the most part, sexual dimorphism is probably the result of ecological adaptation (Crook & Gartlan, 1966).

If we cannot draw any simple unilinear evolutionary conclusions from the primate record, what can we infer from simian species to ours? First, relations of dominance between males and females of a given species seem to have a good deal to do with the relative size, and hence strength, of the sexes. Gibbons, which have little or no sexual dimorphism, have egalitarian sex relations, and so do the chimpanzees, which have moderate dimorphism. Gorillas, whose males are much larger than females, have clearly male-dominated societies, although their peaceful disposition renders male domination relatively benign. The highly dimorphic and aggressive baboons and macaques have strongly male-dominated societies. The inference for man is that, although his moderate dimorphism probably constitutes an important morphological basis for the ubiquity of male domination in human societies, yet that dimorphism is not so great that it should make a chimp-type, egalitarian solution unthinkable.

Second, there is an obvious relationship between erotic and mating behavior, and aggression and dominance behaviors. Among a number of baboon species, for example, "presenting" behavior is exhibited not only by females toward males, but also by subordinate males toward dominant ones. Similarly, in the squirrel monkey, penile display is practiced between males to establish or confirm dominance-submission relationships as well as in heterosexual courting behavior. The dominant male monkey spreads his legs and thrusts his erected penis almost into the face of the subordinate male, attacking him if the subordinate animal does not remain quietly submissive (Maclean, 1965). The use of "obscene" language and gestures in dominance displays between American males is an obvious human parallel. In any case, the intimate link between sexuality, gender dominance, age dominance, and other forms of structured inequality is evident. It seems gratuitous to invoke elaborate psychoanalytic interpretations of "penis envy" or sadomasochism to account for what is simply the extension of sexual posturing to nonerotic forms of dominance relationships among humans. Tiger and Fox (1971), however, suggest that dominance in terrestrial primates is a path to reproduction, or that politics in its broadest and most fundamental sense (of dominance relations) is genetics. The more dominant males are, the more they mate.

Third, there is no such thing as "primate social organization." The range of behavior among species is enormous. Some species are territorial, others are not; some are tightly organized and tyrannical, others loose and permissive; some are sexually promiscuous, others monogamous, yet others polygynous; some are male dominated, others sexually egalitarian; some are gregarious, others introverted and solitary; some have a minimal nuclear family social structure, others have a complex multileveled one. The continuum from the gibbon to the hamadryas baboon, for example, is extremely wide on a number of dimensions, and there are many gradations in between. Closely related species of baboons and macaques have broadly similar societies, but biological relatedness to man does not imply humanlike social organization. Thus, we may conclude that the social evolution of primates consists of divergent and often highly specialized adaptations to specific environments: some are arboreal, some terrestrial; some are adapted to rain forest, others to semidesert; some are vegetarian, others omnivorous. These environmental adaptations affect not only anatomical characteristics such as limb length or tooth structure, but also social behavior.

Fourth, in one important respect, however, all primates are alike, namely in the strength of the mother-infant tie. Clinging to the mother is a widespread behavior pattern of primate infants (Bowlby, 1969). This generalization includes humans and is actually a mammalian characteristic, but the especially long period of primate dependency accentuates this mammalian trait. The Harlow's experiments (1965) on maternal deprivation have documented the crucial importance of infant-mother ties for the normal development of rhesus monkeys. Van Lawick-Goodall (1967, 1968) reports life-long ties of recognition between chimpanzee mothers and offspring, well beyond the dependency period. Copulation between subhuman primate fathers and daughters or siblings seems uninhibited, but not between mothers and sons. Even the orangutan, that least social of primates, preserves the mother-infant tie as the minimal condition for survival.

Fifth, there is a good deal of *intraspecific* uniformity of behavior in the social behavior of primates. Primates of a given species, though also adaptable to change, will tend to reproduce in captivity some of the behavior patterns they exhibit in the wild. Of course, it is possible to modify primate behavior drastically through conditioning experiments. It is easy to produce socially inept and psychologically neurotic monkeys by raising them in an *asocial* environment (Harlow, 1965; Harlow & Harlow, 1965). The same effect can be achieved just as devastatingly with humans, as any policeman versed in the technique of solitary confinement well knows. Harlow (1965) demonstrated, for example, that rhesus monkeys deprived of contacts with mothers and age peers during infancy were almost without exception unable to achieve a successful copulatory position.[3] But, if zoo conditions allow a sufficient number of

---

[3] The early age at which deprivation of social contacts produces seemingly irreversible damage in the rhesus monkey's ability to behave normally raises the interesting subject of *imprinting* in primates. The phenomenon of imprinting reported in birds and other animals is still imperfectly understood; it cannot be explained satisfactorily either as pure heredity or as learning. It seems that certain behaviors fail to develop if, during a very circumscribed "critical period" during maturation, the animal is not exposed to a suitable stimulus. The "following" behavior of young geese is an example of imprinting. Such phenomena are better described as environmental conditions that provide a necessary trigger for genetic predispositions rather than as learning in the conventional sense. For example, in bird experiments, inanimate objects or humans were found to be adequate substitutes for a live mother goose—the young geese deprived of a mother learned to trail after the human experimenter, just as they would have imprinted on their mother (Lorenz, 1952).

animals of a given species to live together so as to approximate their normal group size in the wild, and if blatant forms of experimental compulsion (such as maternal deprivation or isolation from other members of the species) are lacking, the captive monkeys will exhibit forms of behavior characteristic of their species, except that the confining and impoverished environment of a zoo may produce stereotyped and repetitive mannerisms not exhibited in the wild. The obvious inference here is that the social behavior of primates is, at least in part, conditioned by genetic predispositions.

This conclusion must be qualified by a sixth observation, however. Compared to other mammals, primates show greater *intraspecific* plasticity of social behavior, and as among primate species, there seems to be a general evolution from monkey, to apes, to man. Several primate species have been induced to change their behavior in the wild through experimental changes introduced by man.

Unfortunately, not enough experimentation has been made with wild primates to determine accurately the scope of their ability to transmit learning socially, that is, to develop the rudiments of culture. We know, of course, that individual monkeys can learn a wide repertoire of behavior, but, for lack of experimentation, we may underrate their ability to transmit culture. Among two bands of Japanese macaques, for example, the social transmission of learned behavior has been established. One band developed a "swimming culture" after some individuals had been attracted to the water by means of artificial feeding. The whole band later began to swim as a collective "sport." Another band responded to being fed on the sandy seashore by learning to transport food to the water (using extensive bipedalism while carrying the food) in order to wash it. There, too, the intervention spread through social learning. Goodall found that the artificial feeding of wild chimpanzees markedly affected their social behavior. When she fed them a big pile of bananas in one location, the normally unaggressive, egalitarian chimps became suddenly aggressive and exerted dominance behavior. Dominant animals even hoarded the suddenly abundant food in a striking simian confirmation of the Marxian thesis that the accumulation of surplus is the origin of social inequality (National Geographic Society, 1971).

Kummer (1968) suggests ecological adaptation as the explanation for the size of groups in the Hamadryas baboon, and Rowell (1969) reports a group of *Papio anubis* baboons in Uganda which, unlike the same species studied by De Vore and Washburn, does not have a stable hierarchy nor even unit membership of adult males, and has a random marching order when foraging. Rowell gives an ecological explanation for these behavioral differences in the Uganda baboons, linking the lack of hierarchy with the seeming absence of predation (the preying of larger animals on smaller), thus making dominance behavior and strict social organization unnecessary. Behavioral modification in primates, then, does not seem restricted to changes introduced by man, but covers a wide range of ecological adaptations.

Summarizing the results of his own studies on two species of New World monkeys, and of other field and experimental studies, Mason (1971) questions the earlier assumption made by a number of primatologists that, "each primate species had a characteristic social structure." His conclusions make room for both genetic predisposition of social behavior and for intraspecific variation:

Although each species seems to favor certain patterns of social organization, intraspecific variation is considerable. Recent findings indicate that the differences in social structure between two populations of the same species from contrasting locations may be almost as large as that between two populations of different species. Clearly, a single pattern of social organization can no longer be regarded as a fixed, species-typical trait. Nevertheless, it seems likely that each species is in fact predisposed toward certain forms of social organization. . . .

Primates in captivity give clues also of the evolutionary tendency for the more intelligent animals to exhibit greater plasticity in behavior. Apes in captivity show a markedly greater degree of behavioral modification than do monkeys; for example, in the imaginativeness of their sex play, or in using man-made objects placed at their disposal as toys or tools. Among apes, the chimpanzee appears the most human in this respect, whereas the captive gibbon behaves in a more rigidly stereotyped way more reminiscent of monkeys. Man's behavior is, of course, more adaptable than even the chimpanzee's, but to jump from that conclusion to a facile rejection of *any* genetic determinism of human social behavior is clearly unwarranted. The ethnographic evidence certainly makes it possible to entertain as hypotheses that man is *by nature* a territorial,[4] aggressive,[5] age-graded, male- and adult-dominant, and

---

[4]The phenomenon of territoriality is not as simple and as uniform as it is often implied to be, as Ardrey (1966), for example, suggests. The term *territoriality* covers a wide range of behavior which, although relatively fixed within a species, varies greatly from species to species (Klopfer, 1968).

[5]Among those who accept the fact that *Homo sapiens* is an extraordinarily aggressive animal, there is wide disagreement

polygynous (that is, neither monogamous nor promiscuous) animal. Even if one admits that from even the most adaptable of apes to man there is an increase in modifiability of behavior, it does not by any means follow that genetic determination of behavior suddenly vanishes. In fact, it almost certainly does not vanish even though the significance of genetic determination is reduced. Conversely, the great jump from nature to culture that was supposed to set us apart from other primates is not nearly as much a human monopoly as was once believed. We are not as unique as we once thought in our ability to transmit learned behavior. Both culturally and biologically, a comparative study of primates reveals a behavioral gradient from monkeys, to apes, to humans, rather than any sharp discontinuities.

Finally, all primates, including man, have some role differentiation based on age and sex. For the less sociable primates, such as orangutans and gibbons, this differentiation is less pronounced, but for the more complexly organized species, such as baboons, sex and age differences in roles and in behavior constitute the basis of their social system (Kummer, 1971; Mason, 1971). In most species, sex dimorphism and age

---

concerning the evolutionary roots of this aggression. Some, like Ardrey, argue that aggressiveness was an evolutionary adaptation that occurred when paleolithic hunters became, in effect, "killer apes," that is, hunters and scavengers. Man-the-hunter, they claim, was selectively bred for ferocity. This explanation is not very convincing because man is far from unique as a predator on other species. The concept of aggression acquires meaning only when it is restricted to behavior directed against members of the same species. The uniqueness or near uniqueness of man lies in his ferocity to cospecifics (members of his own species), a phenomenon not satisfactorily explained by the man-the-hunter hypothesis. Lorenz (1966) suggests that animals (such as wolves or lions) that are biologically equipped to do grievous bodily harm to members of their own species develop an inborn inhibition against intraspecific aggression, whereas biologically ill-armed animals do not. Man, being in the latter category, became his own worst enemy when his intelligence enabled him to develop lethal weapons without possessing the inborn inhibition against using them against cospecifics. Leakey leans to a different interpretation yet. He claims that it was the humanization of man, and especially the development of abstract speech in the last quarter-million years or so of hominid evolution, which turned man against man. The characteristic of human aggression, says Leakey, is not only that it is intraspecific, but that it is organized and premeditated. This takes abstract speech.

polymorphism are well marked, and there seems to be a fairly close association between these physical differences and the extent to which age and sex roles are sharply defined. In general, reproduction and nurturance are the nearly exclusive province of females, whereas protection is the main role of males. The closely protective and nurturing mother-infant relationship seems to be one of the more universal features of primate societies, though it is, of course, not limited to primates (Sade, 1965; van Lawick-Goodall, 1967, 1968; Rosenblum, 1971). Age polymorphism creates clearly visible age grades in a number of species. Each age grade behaves and is responded to in well-differentiated ways. Infants are generally helpless for several months and are treated gently and tolerantly by older animals. They remain close to their mothers until weaned, a period which may last two or three years. Thereafter, the young tend to congregate in bands of age peers, especially in species in which births are seasonal. The onset of puberty, marked by visible physiological changes in both sexes, such as genital swellings for females in oestrus and continued growth in size for males, brings again distinct behavioral changes, not only in the obvious onset of copulation, but also in the young adults' relationships to older adults of both sexes. Young males previously tolerated by older males, for example become sexual competitors and are pushed out to the periphery of the group. Hair color may further distinguish between younger and older adults, resulting in further role differentiation, as among hamadryas baboons and gorillas.

Our survey of some higher primates, though far from exhaustive, clearly shows that age and sex differentiation, as fundamental bases of social organization, are universal not only to human, but to primate societies. To some degree, this is true for most higher mammals. Furthermore, it seems that the social importance of age and sex differentiation varies directly both with the degree of biological differences between age and sex groups, and with the degree of complexity of the social organization. In fact, among nonhuman primates, age and sex differences are the main principles of social organization; for females, the only other factor of substantial significance is the stage of the reproductive cycle in which they find themselves (anoestrus, oestrus, pregnancy, lactation).

The inescapable conclusion is that differentiation of social behavior by age and sex among humans is part of our biological heritage as primates, however much culture may have modified, elaborated on, or in some cases reduced the practical significance of these differences. Our relatively great longevity and slow maturation have enhanced the importance of age differentiation. Along with other terrestrial primates, our survival has dictated gender specialization in the nurturing and protecting functions. In fact, gender specialization among humans has proceeded further than among other primates that are overwhelmingly foragers. As we became more adept killer-apes, it was the male of the species who brought home the bacon, while the female remained the virtually exclusive caretaker of infants. Bowlby (1969) makes a strong case for the *phylogenetic development* of mother-child "attachment behavior." As hunters (which we were during all but the last few thousand years of our history), we also learned to share food, perhaps one of our most significant leaps on the road to humanity. Whatever else we did, we also developed and specialized as a *biological species* uniquely adapted to an ecological niche. It is logical, therefore, that we turn next to the human biology of age and sex.

3 The Human Biology of Age and Sex

For several generations, the nature-nurture debate has raged between biological and social determinism of human behavior. Our self-imposed ethical limitations on experimentation with humans make it difficult to define precisely the parameters of human behavior. But, at least two things should be clear by now. First, defining the problem as a simple dichotomy between heredity and environment, or nature and nurture, is more limiting than useful.[1] Second, social scientists can continue to disregard human biology only at their own peril.

Human behavior is almost invariably the product of a complex interplay between at least three major classes of phenomena:

---

[1] A recent exchange on the subject is found in Lorenz (1965) and Lehrman (1970). Lorenz takes Lehrman, Schneirla (1956), and others whom he calls the "behaviorists" to task for overstating the influence of learning and understating species-specific, innate predispositions in explaining human and animal behavior. Lehrman replies that much of the confusion in the heridity-environment debate arises from a dual usage of the term *innate* or *inherited*. It is one thing, says Lehrman, to speak of the genetic constitution of an organism, or of change through genetic selection in a population as hereditary or innate factors. It is quite another matter, however, to assume that a given genetic constitution leads to *developmental fixity* in behavior. The same genetic makeup may, under different environmental conditions, lead to different phenotypes. Conversely, an environmental change that may affect the phenotypic development of one genetic constitution may leave another unaffected. The interplay, says Lehrman, is not between heredity and environment, but between an *organism* and its environment.

We are the product of our biology, of our physical environment, and of our social environment. (What we call *psychology* is probably reducible to the range of individual variation that results from the interplay of the three major classes of influences and thus is not accorded separate status here.) Our biology is in good part genetically transmitted, but it is also modifiable through both our physical and social environments. Our social environment, extraordinarily self-determined and modifiable compared to that of any other species, is nevertheless subject to the constraints of both our biology and our physical environment. Unfortunately, the term *ecology* has been used loosely to mean man's adaptation to his physical environment both as a biological organism and as a social being, thereby covering a wide range of phenomena. Unfortunately, too, there is no generally accepted label to cover the study of the relationship between human biology and society, although some approaches in psychology, notably psychoanalysis, have analyzed problems in those terms, with rather limited success. We might perhaps suggest *biosociology*.

One class of phenomena is especially interesting and relevant to the topic of sex differentiation. Called *imprinting* or *critical period phenomena* by animal ethologists, certain forms of behavior seem to be triggered by a special interplay of biology and environment. Broadly, imprinting refers to behavior that is established quickly and "naturally" during a limited critical period in the maturation process of the organism. If established during that critical period, the behavior is irreversible or at least very difficult to extinguish; the same behavior is also extremely difficult to establish either before or after the critical period. Precise and species-specific (characteristic of a particular species) biological predispositions are necessary, but not sufficient, conditions for the behavior to be established. An environmental "trigger" also must be present. Thus, newborn chicks can be imprinted to follow almost any moving object within limits of size and speed, and once imprinted on a given object cannot be made to follow a hen. In humans, it seems that learning both speech and gender roles is analogous to imprinting (Money, 1965; Lenneberg, 1967). As far as we know, in all societies, speech and gender roles are acquired simultaneously, universally (except for the mentally subnormal), and almost irreversibly during the second year of life.

Man's sociability makes it practically impossible to separate the effects of nature and culture on his behavior. We know next to nothing of what a completely asocial man would be like. There are practically no authenticated cases of truly "feral" humans raised with no contact with other humans. We do have considerable evidence, however, on the effect of impoverishing the social environment: it is devastating, and, the longer and the earlier an impoverished environment is introduced, the more extensive and irreversible the damage. Evidence from primate experiments (Harlow, 1965), from human infants raised institutionally, and from police state practices clearly indicates that deprivation of social contact is one of the most severe forms of punishment for adults, and would in all likelihood produce catatonic imbeciles if imposed in early childhood.

Thus, we are fairly certain that some social environment is a necessary condition for the development of virtually all "normal" human behavior, including some acts that we often consider innate or "instinctive," such as mating. Yet, a social environment is not a sufficient condition for developing normal behavior. A chimpanzee raised by loving humans becomes at best a caricature of man; human nurturance does not make the chimpanzee a man, nor even a "better" chimpanzee, but a creature inept in both species. Conversely, any human of normal intelligence, if transplanted in infancy into any culture, can learn to become a competent member of his adopted group. The transplanted individual may, of course, be socially stigmatized because of his foreign origin or, in racially conscious societies, because of his physical appearance. This, however, has nothing to do intrinsically with biology, but only with the social importance that some societies attribute to superficial physical characteristics. When the transplanted individual is treated decently, adaptation to the new culture is unproblematic. In fact, humans seem to retain great flexibility of cultural adaptation until adolescence, as shown by countless examples of individuals raised in societies other than those of their birth.

These facts show two things: first, it takes an organism of the species *Homo sapiens* to make a human; second, it takes more than one, and probably several members of both sexes, and both adults and children to produce a human society. It seems doubtful that two infants of opposite sexes raised in a soundproof, windowless, blank cell could, in total isolation from other humans, independently reproduce a recognizably human society. They might not even learn to copulate, much less be able to acquire a language.

For all his extraordinary (by comparison with other species) behavioral plasticity, man remains recognizably and undeniably human in all societies. Humanity is clearly a product of the complex interaction of heredity and environment. Very few individuals would choose solitude or the company of other animals over social intercourse with fellow humans, however culturally alien they might be. Considering the uncertainty of one's reception in an alien group, this is no trivial fact. We even have cases from North and South American cannibalistic groups, such as the Tupi, Huron, and Creek, in which war captives did not seek to flee even though they knowingly faced the almost certain prospect of being eaten after a period of a few months or years among their captors. Of course, the reason they did not flee was not that they actively enjoyed the company of their captors; rather, they were conditioned to bear adversity with fortitude, or else to suffer disgrace and ostracism in their own group. The fact remains, however, that even the prospect of being eaten was not sufficient incentive to opt for life as an outcast.

The starting point of our inquiry into the human biology of age and sex is this: genetically transmitted physiology and morphology can be considered a substratum of predispositions that set broad but definite limits on human behavior. Any rigidly deterministic theory of biological conditioning of human behavior is obviously inadequate, but equally inadequate is the other extreme, so popular in social science until recently—rejecting biology as largely irrelevant to an explanation of social events in general, and age and sex differences in particular.

We know, at least in a gross way, what main physiological and morphological changes take place with maturation and aging, although we do not know the causes of aging and there is still considerable argument over the extent to which these changes affect behavior. In Cannon's words (1932), "As organisms grow older they manifest an increasing tendency to be indolent." Growing old is a gradual process of declining energy; lowering of the basal metabolic rate; decreasing strength, memory, and recuperative ability; and progressive deterioration of the basic homeostatic mechanisms that give us the relative freedom, which mammals enjoy, from the constraints of the external environment. We gradually decline in our ability to adjust to heat and cold (and our internal temperature declines slightly with age), to store and use glucose, to control blood acidity, to expand and contract our blood vessels, and to have our heart respond to strain by a faster beat.

According to Shock (1962b), the average 75-year-old man has about 90 percent of a 30-year-old's nerve conduction velocity, 88 percent of his body weight, 84 percent of his basal metabolic rate, 82 percent of his body water content, 80 percent of his blood flow to the brain, 70 percent of his cardiac output at rest, 56 percent of his brain weight, 55 percent of his hand grip strength, 50 percent of his kidney plasma flow, 43 percent of his maximum breathing capacity, and 40 percent of his maximum work rate for short bursts. Interestingly, a number of these biological functions seem to decline at a fairly constant rate from around age 30 (Riley & Foner, 1968). The basic mechanism that causes this decline seems to be the death of individual cells.[2] After reaching adulthood, we lose cells more quickly than we can replace them (Shock, 1962b).

The effects of aging on muscular strength, arteriosclerosis, endocrine gland functions, sexual potency in males, visual and auditory thresholds, sensorimotor reaction times, and other easily measurable functions are obvious enough. The evidence on intellectual functions, however, is less clear, and interpretations vary widely. Psychologists disagree on the nature of intelligence, and, if they agree on anything, it is on the inadequacy of I.Q. tests to measure the biological component of intelligence unaffected by environmental influences. Cross-sectional studies of intelligence, which compare different age groups at a given time, show that test scores reach a peak in the late teens or early twenties and decline ever after (Riley & Foner, 1968). However, longitudinal studies of the same persons at successive periods of their lives do not show such a steady overall decline, at least not until age sixty or so. Even past sixty, the decreases shown in longitudinal studies are not as great as those shown in cross-sectional studies.

The discrepancy between the two types of studies is misleading, however. Cross-sectional studies do not take into account the rising level of education of the society over time, and thus compare groups that are not only disparate in age but also in environmental circumstances. It is little wonder, then, that age differences in I.Q. test scores are magnified. Longitudinal studies are far more accurate in this respect, since they test the same individuals over time. While these studies tend to show no appreciable decline in *overall* I.Q. test performance until senescence, this overall stability seems to result from two contradictory trends: the more biologically determined components of intelligence, such as memory (especially short-term memory) and learning ability, do indeed steadily decrease from early adulthood, whereas the environmentally determined factors of verbal ability and general information continue to increase through middle age. That is, we continue to learn and retain facts and thus to accumulate knowledge through later adulthood, but we do so at a steadily diminishing pace and with dwindling efficiency. Our biological

---

[2]Of course, to say that the senescence of an organism is the result of cellular death rates does not explain the ultimate causes of why the cells themselves age and die. There are a number of theories about the ultimate causes of senescence, but relatively little firm evidence. Senescence has been attributed to the accumulation of waste products in tissues, to the development of autoimmunity caused by antibodies responding to cell mutations, and to cell mutations themselves (most of which are deleterious).

capacity to learn declines early, a fact confirmed by the irreversibility of nerve cell losses, the brain's steady weight loss (down to one-half its early adult weight), the drastic shrinkage of the cerebral cortex, and other obvious morphological changes. Since I.Q. tests also measure to a large extent acquired knowledge, the biological effects of aging on intelligence are masked, however. (Masking real biological changes by I.Q. tests is the precise obverse of the spurious "racial" differences shown by the same tests.)

In short, aging basically means diminishing elasticity, a process that begins practically at birth, and from early adulthood includes diminishing strength, fertility (and sexual potency for males), sensorimotor skills, memory, learning, and practically every other basic biological ability.

Several important qualifications that modify the social significance of the physiology of aging should be introduced. First, the rate of decline is not the same for all organ systems; some functions become more quickly impaired than others. Since the rate of decline, though often fairly constant in a given organ, varies from organ to organ, the overall coordination among organ systems tends to break down at an increasing pace in later (as opposed to earlier) adulthood (Shock, 1962*b*). Tasks requiring complex sensorimotor coordination may show rapid deterioration with senility, after a long period of slow and barely perceptible decline. Also, we enter early adulthood with sufficient cellular surplus that our earlier cellular losses are insignificant in impairing performance.

Second, there is a great deal of individual variation in the rate of aging, and much of that variation is environmentally rather than physiologically determined. Diet, amount of physical exercise, incidence of pregnancies, disease, and accidents are among the factors that appreciably affect individual rates of aging. Among the blessings of advanced technology are not only greater longevity but delayed senescence. Within societies, access to such social resources as power and wealth results in substantial class-based differences in the rate of aging as well as in life expectancy.

The effect of aging on intelligence, in particular, reveals a wide range of individual variation. Intellectual decline with age is pronounced among those with lower I.Q.'s (insofar as tests accurately measure intelligence) but, slight and insignificant until an advanced age among those who scored high in youth. We should note, however, that even for those at the high end of the I.Q. spectrum, some intellectual skills decline with age, as shown by the precocity of famous mathematicians and physicists, for example.

Most important, the fact that so much of human behavior is learned diminishes the social relevance of biological decline. To a large degree, experience and knowledge make up for declining physical powers and intelligence. In no known society does the peak of social status coincide with the peak of physical condition. The English expression "prime of life," for example, refers to a social and not a physical condition, and Western societies are typical in allocating the bulk of power and wealth to persons well into the second and physically declining half of their life cycles. True gerontocracies are exceptional, but late middle age is the typical locus of social power in most societies. Some societies, such as the United States, idealize youth, and there is perhaps a tendency to reduce by a few years the mean age of the wielders of power in advanced industrial societies, in which the pace of technological change accelerates the rate of skill obsolescence. Thus, in the United States, the men in power are perhaps a decade or so younger than the rulers in France or Britain, but they are still typically a quarter of a century past their physical prime.

Even in athletics, where the premium on youth is most blatant, the training of athletes is typically controlled by persons who have aged hopelessly beyond competitive range. People in their twenties do the running, but they are being run by trainers in their forties or fifties. Of course, the same is true in warfare, another field of activity in which physical prime is at a premium: while young men do the killing and the dying, older men tell them how, when, and where.

This state of affairs is often actively resented by younger people; nevertheless, the young are seldom able to overthrow the older generation because older (but not senile) people are able to compensate loss of vigor and intelligence with the experience and knowledge through which they control key resources. Ironically, even when "young Turks" overthrow "old guards," the new ruling group is typically made up of the older of the young Turks. Thus, graduate students and not freshmen dominate student politics in the United States. The far more common type of generational "changing of the guard," however, occurs when middle-aged persons displace a senescent group rather than when young people push aside middle-aged ones. For example, the vice-president of a company is likely to be ten to twenty years younger than the president he replaces, not thirty to forty years younger.

Physiology clearly plays an important role in the distribution of power, but it is always mediated through social factors. Sheer physical strength gives adults an enormous advantage over children, and men somewhat of an advantage over women, but any theory of power that reduces its explanation to physical advantage of size and strength is obviously insufficient to account for most human behavior.

At least as important for an understanding of human behavior as the process of aging among adults is the physiology of maturation during pre-adulthood. The biological constraints on human behavior are narrower during childhood than at any time during adulthood, except during the advanced stages of senility. No sane individual, for example, would contemplate putting a five-year-old, however healthy and intelligent, in the cockpit of a jet airplane, even if the plane could be reduced in scale to put all commands at his fingertips. Such physiologically determined factors as need for sleep and attention span, for example, would present insuperable barriers to adequate performance.

During infancy, biology places severe limits on learning. Human infants, although able to track light signals at birth, take several weeks to achieve good binocular vision. Central nervous system control over the muscles that regulate urination and defecation takes several months to establish, and even the most frantic and punitive parental attempts to accelerate the process meet with limited success. Locomotion and speech, perhaps the two most crucial determinants of social effectiveness, are long delayed in human infants. Crawling takes about six months to develop, but unaided bipedalism typically takes a year. Not until the second year of life does vocalization gradually assume the character of speech, and although environmental conditions, such as contact with adults and older children, can affect the speed of learning, there are clear upper limits to environmental effects. Development can be drastically retarded by impoverishing the environment, but it is difficult to accelerate it much. Beyond infancy, physiological constraints become more flexible and socialization becomes a much more potent determinant of behavior; nevertheless, children's behavior continues to be differentiated from that of adults in part through physiology. The level of kinetic activity and play behavior, for example, is much higher for children than for adults, as is also true for primates, cats, dogs, and countless other mammals.

Another interesting but poorly understood aspect of human maturation is the uniquely human phenomenon of *hemispheric dominance* and *lateralization of function* in the brain. In humans, one cerebral hemisphere, generally the left one, is more developed than the other and more closely linked with such functions as speech and motor skills. This asymmetry is absent at birth but emerges very early in the maturation process (Lenneberg, 1967).

Regarding physiological differences by gender, the effects of biology and social environment are once again so empirically intertwined that categorical answers are difficult. To start at the beginning, the sex of a human embryo is normally determined by its father, whose sperm can contribute either a Y (male) or an X (female) chromosome to the X chromosome egg. X chromosomes are considerably larger and contain more genes than Y chromosomes, a factor that accounts for the incidence of such sex-linked traits as color blindness, hemophilia, and heriditary baldness (Harrison, 1964). Many of these traits, however, are genetically recessive.

Of course, recessive genes are not confined to the X chromosome, and most of them are not sex-linked at all. In the normal diploid individual, chromosomes and their constituent genes (*genes* are the units of heredity carried by the chromosomes) are paired off; physical traits are determined by one or more pairs of genes. A *recessive* gene is a gene whose characteristics are not manifest in the individual when paired with a *dominant* gene, but only when paired with another recessive gene. A *dominant* gene is one that masks the visible effect of its paired recessive gene. A person's *phenotype* refers to his outward appearance; his phenotype may or may not be the same as his *genotype*, or his genetic makeup. For example, a person carrying two dominant genes for brown eyes is said to be *homozygous* (having identical genes) dominant, and will be brown-eyed both phenotypically and genotypically. A blue-eyed person is necessarily homozygous recessive, and here again phenotype and genotype coincide. A *heterozygous* (having two different genes) person, however, carrying a blue-eyed gene from one chromosome and a brown-eyed gene from another, will be phenotypically indistinguishable from a homozygous dominant brown-eyed person. His phenotype is dominant, but his genotype is heterozygous, and he will transmit recessive (blue-eyed) genes to half his offspring.

The peculiarity of the sex-linked characteristics is that they are determined by genes on the X chromosome that are lacking on the Y chromosome. Thus, a female who has two X chromosomes needs a recessive gene on each of these for a given recessive trait to show itself, whereas a male is phenotypically recessive if he carries the recessive gene on his one X chromosome. Females have only the square of the probability of males to be phenotypically recessive. (The probability of an independent event's happening twice is the square of the probability of its happening once. Thus, a head on two successive coin flips will happen, on the average, one time out of four, because the probability of its happening on any single throw is one-half.) If, say, the recessive gene for color blindness is present in one in twenty of a population's X chromosomes, one in twenty of the males in that population will be color blind, compared to only one in 400 of the females.

Since a good many of these recessive genes are deleterious, and since females can be protected from the effect of a sex-linked recessive gene through a heterozygous genotype, the sex chromosomes may go a long way in explaining the consistently higher mortality of males in all age categories, and hence the appreciably greater longevity of females. In their resistance to most diseases (with some exceptions like breast cancer and gonorrhea) females are the superior organism. Although for most of history, young women had higher death rates than young men, this was due principally to death in childbirth. Now that death from childbirth has been enormously reduced, women in industrialized countries are living longer than men. Disease resistance may be affected by genetic makeup, and that in turn may be related to the sex chromosomes, given the greater incidence of harmful sex-linked recessive genes in men.

Other basic but unexplained physiological differences by sex concern basal metabolic rate (BMR) and body temperature. Women have a slightly higher body temperature than do men, and their BMR (expressed in calories per square meter of body surface, thus controlling for size) is consistently some 5 percent lower than that of men.

The most obvious morphological differences between men and women are their reproductive organs and the "secondary sexual characteristics" such as body size, fat-to-muscle ratio, body hair, bone structure, and so on. Compared to other primates, sexual dimorphism in *Homo sapiens* is moderate, and, within the species, the amount of sexual dimorphism varies from group to group. Among the Klamath, an indigenous group of the Northwest coast of North America, for example, males average only two inches taller than females, while among the Shilluk of Sudan, height difference reaches eight inches (D'Andrade, 1966). In percentage, males in some population groups average nearly 9 percent taller than females, while in other groups the difference is only 5 percent (see Table 2). Similarly,

TABLE 2

Male Stature as Percent of Female Stature (by Country)

Country	%	Country	%	Country	%
U.S.	108.5	Ecuador	107.8	Bolivia	106.8
India	108.2	Japan	107.4	Brazil	106.8
Uruguay	108.1	Sweden	107.3	Vietnam	106.8
Malaya	108.0	Chile	107.2	Thailand	106.6
		Burma	107.2	Colombia	105.2

gender differences in amount of body hair are greater among people referred to as Caucasoids than among Negroids or Mongoloids. (Racial groups have little biological significance.)

From primatological evidence, it seems that sexual dimorphism is an environmental adaptation, which, through selective breeding, could be appreciably modified in the relatively short space of a few thousand years. The diminishing biological advantage of sexual dimorphism in man for protection against predators and enemies may well lead to slighter and slighter differences between male and female body size. In fact, space and food shortages in the future may well put a premium on miniaturizing both sexes, much as we have already successfully dwarfed our apartment-dwelling canines. Currently, however, both human sexes are growing bigger, at least in the affluent (and effluent) societies, and we glorify sexual dimorphism in hairiness, body size, and mammary glands.

There is also a relationship between sexual dimorphism and age. As in a number of other primate species, human males take longer than females to reach fully developed adulthood, and the degree of sexual dimorphism increases sharply during adolescence (Figure 1). After reaching a peak in young adulthood, the degree of dimorphism begins to decline after middle age.

We must note also that sexual dimorphism in *Homo sapiens* is not entirely the product of physiology and genetics, but is to some extent affected by social conditions. Physical exercise and diet, both of which may considerably differ between the sexes in a given society, may affect the amount of sexual dimorphism. In some pastoral societies, for example, males have a readier access to dairy products than females, thus giving them a richer diet which may add a couple of inches to their adult height. In industrial societies, sedentary males tend to grow fat and thus to look more like females. A male longshoreman or lumberjack is likely to be more dimorphic than a male bank clerk or a teacher, although, of course, the possibility that larger, stronger men may select to follow these professions accounts for at least part of the differences. Some Soviet female athletes have even managed to reduce sexual dimorphism to the point where their eligibility to compete in the female Olympic events has been challenged by Western countries. In addition to these direct environmental effects we have learned to affect artificially sex physiology through hormones, for example, in the treatment of hermaphroditism.

The sex organs themselves and the physiology of reproduction are obviously different between males and females, but the differences are not as great as they are often thought to be. Embryonic sex differentiation follows a double plan. As far as gonads (testes, ovaries) are concerned, each embryo begins with *Anlagen* ("dispositions") for both sexes, and, as one set of gonads regresses and atrophies, the other proliferates and differentiates (Money, 1965). For the external genitalia, homologous male and female structures (penis, clitoris) differentiate

(Source: Tanner, 1962.)

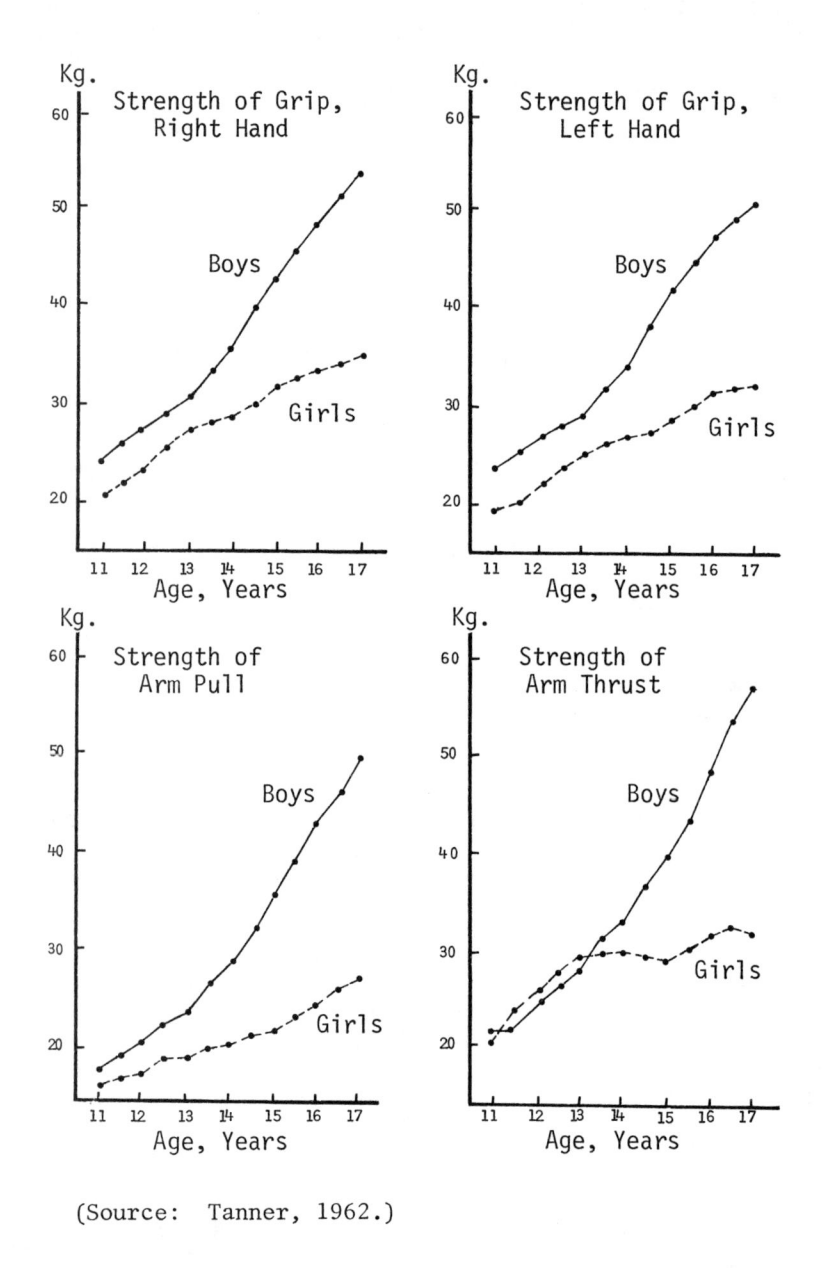

FIGURE 1: Gender Differences in Strength by Age

from the same embryonic *Anlagen*. Experiments with amphibians have successfully reversed genetic sex, and it is not inconceivable that the same could be achieved in mammals, much more complex though they are.

Once formed, the gonads secrete hormonal organizer substances that regulate the differentiation of the remainder of the genital system. It seems, however, that the basic embryonic predisposition in mammals is female, and that male sex is brought about by the addition of something. For example, if embryonic gonads are removed in mammals before genital-duct differentiation, differentiation proceeds as female (Money, 1956).

In fact, sex determination is often not as simple as might appear at first blush. There are numerous hermaphroditic syndromes based on chromosomal anomalies, on the morphology of the external genitalia (such as the adrenogenital syndrome of a female with a penis-sized clitoris and masculine secondary characteristics), and on gonadal abnormalities. Money (1965) finds it necessary to distinguish between genetic sex (as determined by chromosomal composition), hormonal sex (whether predominantly *androgenic* or *estrogenic*), and gonadal sex (ovarian, testicular, or mixed). The majority of individuals in a given population present no sexual ambiguity because all three facets of sex determination are congruent. Nevertheless, embryology, morphology, and physiology all demonstrate that every individual has *Anlagen* for both sexes and continues to secrete both androgen and estrogen. Sex differentiation is basically the tipping of a balance rather than the tossing of a coin.

The sheer physiology of sex differentiation, however, does not tell much about human behavior because that behavior always takes place in a complex environment. As Money rightly states (1965):

The old theoretical dichotomy between the physical and psychological now no longer holds in sex research. . . . Critical-period phenomena demonstrate clearly that development and differentiation may be responsive and adaptive to environmental stimuli during a phylogenetically limited critical period, and then become relatively fixed and immutable, and built into the system. . . . There is no intractable antagonism between psychodynamics or sociodynamics on the one hand, and physiodynamics on the other.

Some sense and a great deal of nonsense have been written about real and alleged gender differences in behavior, including a frequent tendency to attribute these differences to physiology rather than to environmental factors. If, by analogy with racism, we may term "sexist" ideas that attribute socially determined behavior to physiology and genetics, then Western societies and many others as well have been sexist. The

essential difference between race and sex, however, is that the former is a biologically trivial if not meaningless category, whereas the latter is a fundamental one. Thus, to say dogmatically that gender anatomy and physiology are irrelevant to behavior is untenable. In an attempt to disentangle the web of causality, we shall deal in succession with three areas:
1. erotoreproductive behavior
2. character traits and gender roles
3. abilities and skills

Much of the work in sexology has been psychologically and sociologically naïve as well as methodologically sloppy, characteristics epitomized by the pioneering Kinsey reports (1948, 1953). Some of the more recent research has been far more careful and based on directly observed and recorded (as distinguished from reported) behavior (Masters & Johnson, 1965). By now, most of the Freudian conceptions about sexual differences have been relegated to the ethnography of bourgeois, turn-of-the-century Vienna, where they rightly belong. What emerges from the physiological research on erotoreproductive behavior is a mixture of similarities and differences between the sexes, but the emphasis is on the former.

There seems to be general agreement that the androgenic hormones secreted by the adrenal glands regulate the frequency, threshold, and intensity of sexual arousal for both sexes (Money, 1965; Hamburg & Lunde, 1966). The lower, more psychogenic, visual sexual threshold generally reported for males as compared to females may be in part a function of the sex difference in androgen-estrogen balance; but hormonal treatment has shown that both sexes are similarly aroused by the same hormone, androgen, the name of which (meaning *man*) is thus at least a partial misnomer. (Could I suggest *erotogen*?)

Women generally take longer to become aroused and are more dependent than men on tactile stimuli, but the erogenous zones are much the same, localizing in both cases on the external genitalia and more specifically on the anatomically homologous structures of the penis and clitoris. What women "lose" in rapidity and ease of erotic arousal, they "gain" in their far greater ability to experience multiple orgasm during a single act of intercourse, and, conversely, to have intercourse without being sexually aroused at all. Human females are quite exceptional in their lack of a well-defined oestrus; unlike even closely related primates, sexual receptivity in women seems to have a low correlation with probability of impregnation.[3] Another physiological sex difference concerns

---

[3] Of course, it is well known that the body temperature of women rises during ovulation, suggesting perhaps vestigial oestrus. Tiger and Fox (1971) report that women have a greater

the role of the gonads in sexual arousal. Surgical removal of the testes in males reduces sexual response, especially if done before puberty, whereas removal of the ovaries has no such effect in females. In several ways, then, female sexuality can be said to be less closely linked with reproduction than male sexuality.

We must stress that erotoreproductive behavior for both sexes is greatly modifiable through social conditioning, and that many of the actual observable gender differences are the product of social conditioning. Generally, social conditioning of sexuality reinforces and accentuates biological differences, as, for example, in ascribing a more active and aggressive role to males; but, in some cultures, sex role ascription may actually reverse physiological predispositions.

This leads us to the extremely complex question of whether gender differences in character traits have any physiological basis. There is no denying that they are *in part* sociogenic. All societies inculcate sex roles early in the socialization process and there is sufficient cross-cultural variation in such sex roles to dismiss the notion that sex roles are *entirely* physically determined (Mead, 1935, 1949). But, neither can we glibly dismiss *all* biological determination, as some authors come close to doing (Kohlberg, 1966; Mischel, 1966). There is far too much uniformity of findings, not only cross-culturally in *Homo sapiens*, but cross-specifically among primates, to reject biological determinism altogether. Numerous studies of human and nonhuman primates have shown males to be consistently more aggressive and females more dependent and nurturant (Barry, Bacon & Child, 1957; Spiro, 1958; Harlow, 1962; Whiting, 1963; Sears, 1965; D'Andrade, 1966; Seidman, 1966). As we have seen in our survey of subhuman primates, there is a close link between erotic and mating behavior, and dominance-submission relationships. Since the dominant, aggressive male primate is far more likely to impregnate females than are the subordinate males, male primates are selected by evolution for aggressivity (Tiger & Fox, 1971).

Sex differences in temperament appear quite early in infancy—too early, in fact, to attribute them solely to learning. However, in all human societies, sex role ascription begins at or soon after birth, and children typically achieve gender identification between twelve and eighteen months of age, that is, synchronously with the learning of language. Some investigators argue strongly for partial physiological

---

frequency of sexual intercourse around ovulation, and suggest that the greatly increased olfactory sensitivity of women at the time they are most likely to conceive represents a close analog to primate oestrus, albeit in attenuated form.

determination of gender roles (Diamond, 1965); others take a strict behaviorist-learning approach (Mischel, 1966); others yet, while believing that infants are psychosexually neutral at birth, think they acquire irreversible sex identifications quite early in life through a process analogous to imprinting (Money, 1965). The simultaneity of learning gender roles and learning language, and the similarity of both types of learning to "critical period" or imprinting phenomena (Money, 1965; Lenneberg, 1967) strongly suggest a complex interplay between biological and social factors. Sears (1965), while not rejecting the possibility of partial biological determination of gender roles, takes the position that socialization accounts for much of the difference, but notes that, by age three, gender-role differentiation in "styles of aggression" is already "strongly started" in young children.

Cases of hermaphroditism provide tentative and partial answers to the questions. Persons whose sex is physically ambiguous seem to adopt the gender role socially ascribed to them, even if such ascription contradicts their genetic, hormonal, or gonadal sex, provided that their parents or guardians resolve their ambiguity about their offspring's sex (Money, 1965; Hamburg & Lunde, 1966). It is quite possible for persons of unambiguous sex to be ascribed gender roles opposite to their "normal" one. Aggressivity, for example, could be repressed in boys and encouraged in girls. It is foolish to deny the extraordinary potency of learning in humans. Nevertheless, there is considerable evidence for physiological predisposition of gender roles in at least some character traits.

What is at stake is not the feasibility of reversing or neutralizing these predispositions, but rather the social cost of fighting instead of going along with physiology. The empirical rarity of such learned reversals and the virtual absence of sexual *un*differentiation suggest that the cost would be high, or that the cost would not be commensurate with the gain, which amounts to the same thing. Unisex utopians might like to see a society in which gender role differentiation is abolished, and argue that advanced technology brings this prospect within our reach. Empirically, however, the total absence of sexually undifferentiated societies, and the virtual absence of sexually unidentified individuals argue against such a prospect.

We may thus safely conclude with Maccoby (1966) that,
. . . the biological underpinnings of the social demands for sex-typed behavior set modal tendencies for cultural demands, and set limits to the range of variation of these demands from one cultural setting to another. Still, within these limits, considerable variation does occur, between families, between cultures, and in the nature of the behavior that a social group stereotypes as "feminine" or "masculine."

The main effect of social sex-role typing is to elaborate on the physiological *Anlagen*, and to use gender as a basis for dichotomizing much that is biologically neuter. This *social elaboration* on biology is, of course, greatly variable from culture to culture, and, at least in theory, dispensable with.

This leaves us with the subject of sex differences in abilities. Differences in purely physical abilities correlated with size and strength are evident enough and unproblematic. Even the most radical social determinist would concede that size and strength are rooted in morphology and physiology. It is important to note, however, the relatively small magnitude of these sex differences. For any two large and randomly selected groups of men and women, distribution curves would show considerable overlap. Thus, for example, only a small minority of men could match female Olympic records in almost any event, but a few men would be certain to exceed every one of them. This could raise the interesting ideological question of whether a consistent unisex position would lead one to insist on the abolition of sex segregation in sport events, thereby putting women at a severe disadvantage.

Skills and abilities that are not directly based on strength and size are much more problematic. Lacking adequate cross-cultural data, it is almost impossible to establish the causal balance between nature and nurture, insofar as these two terms can be validly opposed in the first place, since culture itself developed out of a process of biological evolution. Summarizing the research (conducted almost exclusively in Western societies), Maccoby (1966) concludes that the data show consistent sex differences both in certain aspects of intellectual performance, and in intercorrelations between such performance and other characteristics. She advances several possible explanations, both physiological and social, but she remains prudently eclectic.

For our purposes, I.Q. tests give us little information, since they have been standardized to minimize sex differences. We do know that girls learn to speak, count, and read earlier than boys, but these differences tend to disappear around age ten; for mathematics, the findings are reversed. This intellectual precocity of girls may be related to their earlier physical and sexual maturation, and probably holds cross-culturally. Other more specific findings, however, are probably culturally determined and limited to Western societies. For example, Maccoby (1966) reports some interesting findings on "cross-sex typing." Children who score high on "analytic thinking, creativity, and high general intelligence" tend to be the more "feminine" boys and the more "masculine" girls. Such findings seem to coincide so closely with specifically Western gender stereotypes and behavioral expectations that they are probably culturally determined.

In short, we can conclude that girls mature physically faster than boys, and that this may well constitute a physiological basis for greater intellectual precocity; but, until we have better cross-cultural evidence, we cannot explain fully the intellectual differences. The gender differences in intellectual abilities that exist in adolescence seem attributable mostly to social factors, and it seems reasonble to hypothesize no significant differences in innate intelligence between males and females.

There is some evidence of physiologically based sex differences in several sensory skills. Women, for example, seem to have a better sense of smell than men; this might be related to the secretion of estrogen, since olfactory acuity for women fluctuates with the menstrual cycle, being at its highest between menses when estrogen production is at its peak (de Groot, 1965). Ovariectomy often results in a decreased sense of smell, but the latter can be restored by administering estrogen (Money, 1965). Another hormone, progesterone, has been shown to enter the brain and to affect brain function, producing anesthesia, sedation, and an elevation of the threshold for convulsive seizures. Hamburg and Lunde (1966) speculate that fluctuations in the level of progesterone during pregnancy and the menstrual cycle may be related to behavioral changes in women at those times.

The abundant folklore in Western societies concerning mood changes accompanying pregnancy and menstruation, while describing phenomena which are, of course, partly sociogenic, should not be facilely dismissed as pure myth, because there are rather striking cross-cultural similarities in this respect. Most of the world's societies subject menstruating women to various taboos ranging from complete seclusion to a prohibition of sexual intercourse. One might argue that behavioral changes are associated with the social stigmatization attached to menstruation, but the specific changes reported show too much cross-cultural similarity for a purely sociogenic interpretation. Davenport (1965), for example, reports that women in a Melanesian group exhibit irritability during menstruation even though they are not subject to strong taboos.

Despite a number of unresolved questions and the great difficulty in separating the effect of nature and nurture in human behavior, we can at least safely conclude that, if we want to understand age and sex differentiation in human societies, we cannot afford to ignore either the human organism or his environment, physical and social. The distinction is artificial: empirical behavior is always a complex blend of physical and social factors. The relative causal weight ascribed to various factors is dictated not so much by behavior in a global sense (at that level of generality, the question becomes nearly meaningless), but by what specific aspects of that behavior we seek to understand. In the remainder of this book, we shall shift the main thrust of our inquiry from the physical to the social realm—that is, we shall ask different questions concerning the same set of phenomena.

4 Sex Differentiation in Human Societies

In all human societies, a person's sex is a matter of considerable social significance, beyond the obvious biological functions of reproduction and lactation. Although calculated, organized protests by groups of women have appeared sporadically for thousands of years in hundreds of societies, the idea that men and women should behave as equals and be treated as such has, so far as we know, been propounded as an articulated ideology only for the last 200 years or so of Western history. Sexual equality is one of the few truly revolutionary ideas in human history, a corollary of the egalitarian ideology of the Enlightenment. Even in Western societies, however, the legal assurance of sexual equality has long been delayed (for example, Switzerland, one of the oldest Western democracies for men, only recently enfranchised women); in fact, relative to men, women in some industrialized Western societies are not better, or are even worse, off than women in a number of nonindustrial societies. Sex inequalities continue to persist and to be widely accepted as legitimate and normal in a number of societies that have long been officially committed to eradicating the harmful effects of other accidents of birth or artifacts of culture.

In assessing the significance of sex differentiation in human societies, we face the problem of striking the correct balance for ourselves between the differences and similarities in the ways other cultures handle the problem. There are some basic uniformities: all societies ascribe distinct roles to men and women; socialize their children into their sex roles early in life, starting in infancy; stigmatize deviance from these roles; and assign some degree of male dominance over women.

Margaret Mead (1935, 1949) has argued that sex-linked differences in character traits, such as aggressivity, submissiveness, and so on, are culturally determined. She produced some ethnographic rarities from New Guinea, in which women and men are as rigidly sex-typed as in Western societies, but in almost a precisely opposite way. She documented other cultures in which sex roles are undifferentiated on some personality dimensions that are considered sex-linked in Western societies. Although Mead did show that sex roles in human societies are extremely varied, she did not establish the existence of a matriarchy, or, for that matter, the absence of sex differentiation in any society. Some early anthropologists, such as Morgan (1877), believed in matriarchy as the original condition of mankind and accepted at face value the social origin myths of many peoples according to which, in the dawn of time, they were ruled by women. The simple fact is that we know of no matriarchal society, past or present. In a few cultures, women are nearly equal to men, and, at the other end of the spectrum, there are societies in which male tyranny is extreme; but females are politically dominant in no known society.

In a few societies, women are erotically aggressive, but that does not make them dominant over men in the political sphere, especially outside the restricted familial group. There are, of course, a number of societies in which individual women have been politically prominent, even to the extent of occupying the supreme office. In recent years, several Asian countries (India, Ceylon, Israel) have had female prime ministers, and the list of famous queens, from Hatshepsut and Cleopatra of ancient Egypt, Catherine the Great of Russia, Wilhelmina of the Netherlands, Maria Theresa of Austria, Tz'u Hsi of China, and Elizabeth I and Elizabeth II of England, is a long one, yet none of these societies ever came close to being matriarchal.

In virtually all societies, men have monopolized or nearly monopolized war, hunting, fishing, and running public affairs, and women have primarily nurtured young children (up to the ages of at least five or six), carried water, gathered fuel, harvested fruits and nuts, and transformed food for general consumption (grinding grain, cooking, preserving meat). The exotic exceptions that anthropologists delight in are, on closer inspection, less deviant than they first appear. For instance, women, especially young childless women, have occasionally been used in warfare. Apart from the ancient Greek Amazon legend, there are a few documented cases of fighting women. Young women fought in the precolonial Dahomeyan army in West Africa, and, of course, modern armies have frequently used women in various auxiliary roles, mostly clerical and medical. This is especially true in periods of large-scale hostilities, when much of the able-bodied male population has been mobilized. Among modern states, Israel, which is in a virtually perpetual state of war, and whose population is greatly outnumbered by the Arabs, has probably gone farthest in mobilizing women, but even in Israel, female soldiers serve in auxiliary, noncombatant roles, and men do nearly all the fighting.

Or, to mention another classical exception, in some South American Indian groups, the father of a newborn infant practices the *couvade* (a French word meaning "hatching"), that is, a show of postpartum incapacitation, but even there the father does not raise the children. As far as hunting is concerned, women of the European nobility sometimes accompanied men on falcon hunts, and even today British females with aristocratic pretensions join their male counterparts in the quaintly anachronistic pastime of chasing foxes through the countryside. Hunting as a pastime of the leisure class is sometimes engaged in by women because the boredom produced by enforced idleness is even more of an occupational hazard for upper-class women than for men, who have at least the distraction of tyrannizing their fellow men. Hunting as a utilitarian and prosaic food-getting activity, however, is almost without exception the province of men.

The basic "biogram" that we inherited from our hunting-and-scavaging hominid ancestors thus still holds: men procure (and share) the meat of large animals and protect the women and children from predators and other men. Women nurture the children, often collect plants and small animals, and prepare the food for common consumption. Weaponry, which alone enabled man to become a successful hunter, also enpowered him to become easily lethal to his own species. The human brain made man his own principal predator, thereby making him both hunter and hunted. The double role of warrior and hunter, and the much older mammalian tie between mother and infant are the evolutionary bedrock of human gender specialization (Bowlby, 1969). Even in the many societies in which hunting is an anachronistic pastime, war is still very much a going concern. As for the dependent lactation of human infants on bovine females, it is too recent a development to have impinged seriously on the mother-infant relationship. Bowlby (1969), for example, reports similar forms of mother-child "attachment behavior" among breast-fed Ganda infants in Uganda as exists among American, Scottish, and English children coming from a bottle-feeding tradition of two or three generations' standing.

Beyond these few uniformities in sex roles, the range of cross-cultural variability in the sexual division of labor is wide indeed. A few generalizations can be made, but they must be extensively qualified. Thus, in pastoralist societies (except in the Andean area of Peru), livestock is typically under the care of males, and in most agricultural societies, the men do the bulk of the heavy work, such as clearing fields. However, in a good number of agricultural societies of central, eastern, and southern Africa, women do most of the farm labor. In many societies that lack domesticated beasts of burden, for example in Africa, women perform the function of carrying heavy burdens, ostensibly to leave men unhampered in their protective role; but in other peasant societies, for example, among Meso-American Indians, members of both sexes carry heavy burdens. Pottery making, being closely associated with cooking food and storing water, is frequently a female specialty, but there are exceptions. The same is true of spinning and weaving, a "spare time" occupation easily conducted at home, but, here too, there are a number of societies in which both men and women weave. Among the Yoruba of southwestern Nigeria, for example, women and men weave two different types of cloth on two different kinds of looms, the women producing strips of eighteen to twenty-four inches in width, the men producing narrow strips of four to six inches. Among Andean Indians also, both men and women weave, but women do most of the spinning. Men almost invariably work metals, make weapons and boats, and frequently build houses. In short, it may be said that women perform tasks that are more sedentary, less arduous, and that do not interfere with child bearing and care, whereas men engage in the more strenuous and dangerous activities (D'Andrade, 1966).

Priestly functions are often the province of men, but the exceptions are numerous, and there are few societies in which some roles having to do with the supernatural are not ascribed to women. Prostitution is predominantly but not exclusively a female occupation.

If one looks at the total amount of productive activity in a given society, there is a distinct relationship between technology and the relative amount of work done by men and women. D'Andrade (1966) distinguishes five basic types of subsistence activity: (1) agriculture with cattle, (2) animal husbandry, (3) agriculture without cattle, (4) fishing and hunting, and (5) gathering. Among these activities, women do a much greater amount of production work in agriculture without cattle societies than in any of the other four types. The amount of productive work is next most equitably distributed in hunting and gathering societies, in which the typical pattern is for men to do most of the hunting and women most of the gathering.

Although within any given society, the division of labor by sex is sharply drawn, most occupations being defined as clearly male or clearly female, there are relatively few specific occupations other than infant care, warfare, and hunting, that are consistently male or female across cultures. Even occupations that require a great deal of brute strength and would thus seem to be more suitable for men are not consistently reserved for males. That the Western conception of women as the "weaker sex" is greatly exaggerated is demonstrated by the regularity with which women do the bulk of the back-breaking labor in a good many peasant societies in Africa and Asia. Sexual dimorphism in humans is not sufficiently pronounced to be a powerful determinant of the sexual division of labor, although child bearing and child care are necessarily determined.

More striking, perhaps, than the wide cross-cultural range of occupational distribution by sex is the fact that nearly all societies have made nearly all of their occupations solely or overwhelmingly monosexual.[1] Some industrial societies have been slightly less rigid in this respect, but even they have shown a high and relatively stable degree of occupational segregation by sex. As far as sex roles are concerned, the tolerance limits are quite narrow, and deviance from accepted norms is typically stigmatized and channelled into low-status roles.

The difficulty and cost of abolishing the sexual division of labor in a given society is illustrated by the limited success of utopian attempts to eradicate occupational gender typing. Spiro (1956), for example, reports on the partial failure of such an attempt in an Israeli Kibbutz (a communal farm). After a period of experimentation in nonsexual task assignment, the Kibbutz reverted to a collectivized version of the traditional division of labor: men engaged predominantly in productive activities and women in service activities. Pregnant women were simply not very good at driving tractors, and it made sense to have nursing mothers close to the nursery rather than away in the fields. Little by little, more and more women found themselves back in the kitchen, laundry, or nursery. The main difference from the surrounding society was that instead of being an unspecialized, unpaid servant for a nuclear family, women were now specialized, unpaid servants to a collectivity of men. Their tasks became more repetitive and boring than before: it is one thing to tend to the myriad of diverse jobs in a household and quite another to spend eight-hour shifts behind a collective kitchen counter or in a nursery.

---

[1] Some authors, in their eagerness to minimize the role of sexual differentiation, have argued that we should really distinguish not between men's work and women's work, but between work that is done by childless and child-rearing adults. There are many societies in which females below and beyond childbearing age are treated in a less sex-differentiated way than fertile females, but none in which a childless adult woman is treated like an adult male and expected to play a male role. Childlessness typically makes the adult female in most societies not more like a man but less than a woman: it entails stigmatization, not "promotion" to male or to "childless adult" status.

Many other radical communal experiments have foundered in the bedrock of sexual differences, and it is probably no accident that the monastic orders of Christianity, Buddhism, and other religions, which have been among the most successful and enduring of communal living groups, have been monosexual. They have solved the problem of relations between men and women by eliminating them altogether. As a fringe benefit, they have not had to worry about child care, unless they chose to specialize in caring for other people's children (orphanages, schools), thereby giving themselves a widely acceptable and this-worldly *raison d'être*, and providing themselves with an alternative mode of self-perpetuation. By drawing recruits from among their wards and pupils, monastic orders developed a nonsexual mode of reproduction for themselves and freed the women of the propertied classes of some of the onus of child rearing.

More recently, the bitter disenchantment of many radical women with bisexual communal living groups and with male-dominated radical political groups, and their strident insistence on sexual separatism (to the extent of advocating lesbianism or at least discouraging emotional involvement with men) point also to the great difficulty of trying to ignore the biologically-based gender differences. Although it remains a moot question whether the source of the difficulty is entirely sociogenic, or partly biological and partly social, experience strongly suggests that the androgynous ideal is unattainable.

The basic mechanism insuring a high degree of sex role conformity is, of course, early socialization. Long before an infant is capable of performing the roles ascribed to either sex, he or she is already strongly channelled along sex lines. The process of sex identification is usually well set in the second year of life. The indomitable human spirit occasionally rebels against this brainwashing. Not all little girls want to play with dolls and serve tea with miniature porcelain sets; some little boys like to knit or to help cook dinner. Most societies find ways of accommodating such deviants, but almost always with some degree of stigmatization. The aggressive woman is a "bitch"; the sensitive man is a "sissy."

Two phenomena of interest here are transvestism and homosexuality; though often linked in Western societies, the two are clearly distinct, sharing only a common deviance from ascribed sex roles.[2] The *transvestite* is a person who expresses

---

[2] Part of the confusion is semantic. Unfortunately, we use the same word in English to refer to gender and to erotic and reproductive behavior. Transvestism has to do with sex-gender; homosexuality is in the realm of sex-eroticism. Obviously, our central concern in this book is with sex-gender, and we are interested in sex-eroticism only insofar as it relates to sex-gender.

a general preference for the role ascribed to the sex opposite to his or her own, and thus frequently dresses and behaves accordingly. Such persons may or may not be homosexuals. *Homosexuals* are persons erotically attracted to members of the same sex; some seek to emulate members of the opposite sex by playing the opposite sex role in a homosexual relationship, but many assume their own sex role and despise the opposite sex. The homosexual frequently deviates from his ascribed sex role only in the choice of sexual partners, while the transvestite has generally rebelled against gender-role ascription.

The range of cultural responses is wide, but, from our fragmentary cross-cultural evidence, it seems that transvestism is more widely stigmatized than homosexuality. In a number of societies, such as ancient Greece, Arab countries, some Melanesian groups (Davenport, 1965), and the Nyakyusa of Tanzania (Wilson, 1951), homosexual behavior is matter-of-factly accepted as either a substitute for or a supplement to heterosexuality. The same is often true in the sex-segregated institutions (such as boarding schools and prisons) of societies that otherwise condemn homosexuality. Homosexuality and bisexuality do not threaten sex role differentiation.

Even in the limited and private sphere of choice of sexual partners, homosexual behavior in many societies that tolerate it does not deviate from gender-role ascription. In a number of these societies, bisexuality is the norm, and homosexuality is a substitute for heterosexuality. Davenport (1965), for example, reports a Melanesian group that tolerates homosexual relations, including anal intercourse between adult male friends (or even brothers), or between adult males and boys aged seven to eleven, but which completely lacks any conception of the exclusive homosexual as a person assigned a special social role. Similarly, Evans-Pritchard (1970) reports acceptance of the custom of "boy marriage" among Zande warriors. Extensive polygyny among the nobility creates a scarcity of marriageable women for young warriors, who have to postpone marriage until their late twenties or thirties, and thus resort to socially accepted pederasty as an alternate sexual outlet. The Western notion of exclusive homosexuality as a form of sexual deviation is probably far less common than matter-of-fact recognition and tolerance of bisexuality.

Social response to transvestism, on the contrary, is almost invariably negative, ranging from ridicule and loss of status to death. Some North American Indian societies institutionalized the role of *berdache* or male transvestite, but in a very marginal way. In ancient Greece and Japan, male actors played female roles in their classical theater, but these are hardly cases of generalized tolerance of transvestism. In Western societies, the stigma has typically been strong. One of the charges that led Joan of Arc to the stake was that she behaved "immodestly." Although her judges unsuccessfully tried to ascribe sexual promiscuity to her, it was evident that she had the audacity of dressing like a man. Her pleas that this was simply a matter of convenience were rejected. Her "immodesty" was one of status, not of eroticism—she did not accept her lowly place as a woman. Even in contemporary Western societies, as indeed in all but the most revolutionary ones (such as Communist China) bent on abolishing sex inequalities, the symbolic importance of sex-linked clothing styles is still apparent. We speak metaphorically of "wearing the pants" to mean "wielding power."

It seems that virtually all societies, not content with the moderate amount of sexual dimorphism with which we are born, further stress sex role differentiation through highly visible social means. Clothing styles stand out most obviously, but even in societies in which nudity or near-nudity is the rule, gender differences are visibly expressed through body adornment such as tatooing, scarification, jewelry, tooth mutilation, and the like.

Interestingly, similar differences in dress and body adornment are also widely used to mark differences in rank or social status. They are then known as "sumptuary regulations." Nevertheless, the widest use of visible symbols of status differences have been applied to sex and to age as the two most widespread bases of social differentiation. Seen in that light, transvestism is clearly a form of social protest, whereas homosexuality is either a last resort, or the expression of a personal penchant. An interesting hypothesis worth testing cross-culturally is that male transvestites are less stigmatized than female ones because the former merely "demote" themselves to female status, whereas the latter challenge male domination and thus threaten the power structure. Indeed, it seems that most cases of institutionalized transvestism, such as the ones mentioned earlier, have involved males playing female roles.[3]

Beyond differences in dress and body adornment, sex roles are also symbolically differentiated in most societies through a combination of rituals, taboos (for example, menstrual or postpartum), spatial segregation (separate sleeping quarters, men's clubs), and rules of etiquette (for instance, "chivalry"

---

[3]Similar phenomena exist in racial caste societies. For instance, in South Africa, a "white" person can much more easily "demote" himself to "colored" status than vice versa. Some whites living maritally with blacks, a punishable crime in South Africa, have opted for racial demotion as a solution to avoid prosecution, and their petitions for reclassification have sometimes been granted.

and "gallantry" in the Western tradition). All these mechanisms are basically means of entrenching a *status hierarchy*, and are also widely used to differentiate invidiously on bases other than sex. Some authors (Tiger, 1969; Tiger & Fox, 1971) have suggested that the organization of males in sex-segregated groups is biologically rooted in the evolutionary history of man as a hunter, but, as groups choose also to segregate themselves on the basis of age, education, class, occupation, ethnicity, "race," and many other invidious distinctions, the sociogenic hypothesis is more plausible. More convincing is the argument by Tiger and Fox (1971) that sex and dominance are closely linked in primates; thus, the tendency of men to organize in sex-segregated and exclusive groups would become an expression of male dominance over females and the young. Male seclusion, like other forms of exclusiveness, would seem to be more the expression of a negative desire to exclude than of a positive bond among men.

So far, we have established the following generalizations about sex role differentiation:
1. It is present in all societies.
2. It is instilled very early in the socialization process, typically in infancy, long before either adult role is to be assumed.
3. It is symbolically expressed through sharply distinct styles of dress and body adornment, and frequently also through rituals, taboos, spatial segregation, and etiquette.
4. It is functionally expressed through a sex-based division of labor in which a few social roles for which the biological advantages of either sex are obvious (war, infant care) are universally or nearly universally ascribed to the same sex.
5. The sexual division of labor is invariably elaborated well beyond the biologically based limitations, each society ascribing most of its occupations solely or overwhelmingly to a single sex.
6. As might be expected, when the sexual division is not rooted in biology, there is little cross-cultural consistency in the ascription of given occupations to either sex.
7. Deviations from socially ascribed sex roles are typically stigmatized by means ranging from ridicule and lowered status to ostracism and death.
8. Although individual women may outrank individual men, men as a group invariably wield more power and status than do women.
9. The degree of disparity between the status of men and women in a given society ranges from near equality to full-blown male tyranny.

Since the hierarchical aspect of sex differentiation is the most consequential in dictating what men and women can and cannot do, we shall now turn our attention to it. More specifically, we shall try to explain what determines the relative degree of inequality between men and women. Given a moderate degree of sexual dimorphism and a basically similar physiology of sex and reproduction throughout the human species, it follows that differences between societies must be sought in the environment, especially in the social environment, rather than in heredity.

For illustrative purposes, let us examine more closely the position of women in relation to men in three societies that, though they are geographical neighbors and indeed intermingle on their fringes, cast their sex roles very differently. We shall look at the Tuareg, the Hausa, and the Yoruba, who occupy respectively the western Sahara, the western Sudan, and the rain forest of coastal West Africa.

The Tuareg are nomads who roam the desert with their camels, donkeys, sheep, and goats (Briggs, 1958; Lhote, 1966). They are Muslims by religion, but marriage is monogamous, unlike nearly all African peoples. Marriage is consecrated by payment of dowry or *bridewealth* (usually seven camels) by the family of the groom to that of the bride. After temporary residence with the bride's parents (*uxorilocal*), the bride resides with her husband and his relatives (*virilocal*).[4] The society is stratified into noblemen, commoners, and slaves, the latter mostly captives from other ethnic groups to the south. The *rule of descent* is an uncommon type known as *double unilineal* from both the mother's female line and the father's male line), political authority being *matrilineally* (in the female line) transmitted.[5]

---

[4]The *rule of residence* in a given society determines who goes where upon marriage; it establishes the composition of the group of relatives who live together. Apart from the rarer possibilities, there are three basic patterns. If husband and wife establish a separate household on marriage, this is known as *neolocal* residence and results in a *nuclear* family composed of spouses and their unmarried children. Neolocal residence, common in the West, is relatively rare elsewhere. By far the most common arrangement is *virilocal* residence (sometimes also called *patrilocal*) whereby the bride joins her husband and his relatives. This leads to an *extended* family composed of at least three generations living together. Much less common is the opposite arrangement, also leading to an extended family, whereby the husband joins his wife and her relatives. This is known as *uxorilocal* residence (sometimes also called *matrilocal*).

[5]The *rule of descent* refers to the genealogical line or lines that are ascribed paramount social significance in a given society. There are two basic possibilities: a few societies

Most visitors to the Tuareg have been astonished at the relatively high status of the women. Some have misleadingly called the Tuareg matriarchal, because authority is matrilineally transmitted. Matrilineal descent and transmission of authority have nothing to do with power being in the hands of women, however. In matrilineal societies, instead of being passed on from father to son, authority is transmitted from mother's brother to sister's son, the woman serving simply as the kinship link between the males of the two succeeding generations. Such is also the case among the Tuareg. Much of the foreign visitors' surprise at the status of Tuareg women resulted from the fact that these visitors came from and expected to find a situation similar to that of Arab Muslims, whose women have a lowly status. The trivial fact that, among Tuareg it is the men whose faces are veiled while the women go barefaced has served to accentuate the contrast between Tuaregs and Arabs.

Tuareg women keep a great deal of independence in marriage and retain control over their own separate property, including camels, the most valuable form of wealth. Women pass on their social status to their sons and assure them their political rights according to the principle of matrilineal inheritance, but women themselves are almost completely excluded from public life. They are treated with the greatest respect and deference but they cannot hold office, appear in council, or even appoint male speakers on their behalf (Briggs, 1958). On rare occasions,

---

recognize equally all lines of descent and are called *bilateral*; by far the greater number of societies give social recognition to only one line of descent and are called *unilineal*. The latter are of two subtypes depending on the sex of the ancestor through whom descent is traced: *matrilineal* and *patrilineal*. Some societies are both matrilineal and patrilineal, a system known as *double descent* or *double unilineal descent*. These societies must not be confused with bilateral descent societies (such as the Western ones). Bilateral descent societies trace descent through the two parents, the four grandparents, the eight great-grandparents, and so on. Double descent societies recognize the father, father's father, father's father's father, etc., *and* the mother, mother's mother, mother's mother's mother, etc., but exclude half of the grandparents, three-fourths of the great-grandparents, etc. The key significance of the unilineal descent is that it creates *lineages* and *clans*, that is, mutually exclusive groups of relatives who share the same socially recognized ancestors. Patrilineal descent tends to go together with virilocal residence, and bilateral descent with neolocal residence, but matrilineal societies may be virilocal, uxorilocal, or, more rarely, "avunculocal."

an older woman of high rank and famous for her intelligence, character, and diplomacy may serve as a mediator in a quarrel; otherwise, women are restricted to the domestic sphere, in which they hold authority over only children and slaves. Inside the tent, segregation prevails: men are seated on the right as one enters, women and children on the left. A woman is free to obtain a divorce by refusing to have sexual relations with her husband and by seeking refuge with her parents. In short, women are respected, listened to, and enjoy an amount of domestic independence, but they are almost entirely excluded from public affairs.

Moving south from the Sahara to the savannah country of the western Sudan, we encounter the Hausa, some twelve million strong, who, for several centuries, have been Islamized and have been organized in agrarian, urbanized, stratified, and politically centralized societies. Their heartlands are the great cities of northern Nigeria, such as Kano, Sokoto, Katsina, and Zaria. Extensively described by M. G. Smith (1955, 1960), Cohen (1969), and others, the Hausa constitute one of the most complex and large-scale societies of Africa, and have been compared to the feudal societies of medieval Europe and Japan. In continuous contact with the Arabs, their Suni Islam is highly orthodox and fundamentalistic, particularly since the early nineteenth-century Holy War led by Usman dan Fodio, who conquered the Hausa states and established Fulani overlordship over them. Unlike most Africans, the Hausa have bilateral descent. Residence is virilocal, and polygyny is greatly esteemed and desired by men. The typical household is a polygynous, virilocal, extended family.

In M. G. Smith's words (1955):

The significant aspect of Hausa sex differentiation is the non-existence of any public role for women. In community social structure, women, as a group, play no part, and have no place except that which kinship or marriage give them, or that which they enter by repudiation of marriage and kinship when they become prostitutes. Even wealthy women who are socially respected remain legal minors . . . politically and legally women are an internally undifferentiated collection of individuals, none of whom are full social persons.

Basically, a Hausa woman has two choices. She can marry, in which case she is said to "steal her own body," that is, to surrender all rights over her body and its issue to her husband. In the upper class, wives are kept in *purdah*, the traditional Muslim seclusion.[6] The ordinary peasant cannot afford the

---

[6]Mary F. Smith (1954) transcribed a detailed autobiographical statement by a Hausa noblewoman, which constitutes one of the most extensive documents on the life of a woman in a traditional African society.

luxury of seclusion for his wife or wives, but, all the same, the Hausa wife is completely under the control of her husband. Only when older, do wives gain some measure of economic independence by being allowed to sell cooked food on the market. Widows are expected to mourn their husband and observe taboos for five months, although widowers are not subjected to the same restrictions. Politically, it seems that the position of women in Hausa society has deteriorated in the last 150 years. Earlier, women could accede to certain titles and political offices from which they are now debarred.

Women do, however, have one escape from their totally dependent marital status. They can obtain a divorce very easily, and in one sample of 477 successful divorce suits (collected by Smith, 1955), women initiated 89.71 percent of them. The main alternative to being a wife, at least for the mass of peasants and commoners, is prostitution, a low-status but not particularly stigmatized occupation. The prostitute is both economically and socially independent of men (Hausa prostitutes apparently do not have pimps). Later, if she has plied her trade successfully and accumulated some money, the prostitute will find suitors and can become a respectable housewife again. Interestingly, only as a prostitute can a Hausa woman play any kind of public social role. She may become a dancer in the spirit-possession (*bori*) cult, a pagan cult associated with prostitutes, and she can become the head of her occupational guild.

Continuing our southbound journey from Hausa country, we come to the Yoruba of southwestern Nigeria, also ten to twelve million strong, highly urbanized since precolonial days, and organized in a multiplicity of city-states and the larger Oyo empire. Under the extensive influence of Islam and Christianity since the early nineteenth century, traditional Yoruba cults continue to flourish, and Yoruba civilization is characterized by an urbane and tolerant religious pluralism. Both Islam and Christianity have become Yorubanized to conform to local customs. The Yoruba, described by Lloyd (1965), Bascom (1970), and many others, are a complex agrarian society with social stratification, an extensive division of labor, elaborate political structures, and a distinguished artistic tradition. Descent is patrilineal, residence is virilocal, polygyny is frequent and highly desired, marriage is by bridewealth, and the residential compound is the standard polygynous, virilocal, extended family so common in Africa.

Yorubaland is extensive enough to show a great deal of internal variation, but in relation to the status of women, the Yoruba stand out among the world's most sexually egalitarian societies. In this respect, the Yoruba resemble many of their neighbors in the coastal forest belt of West Africa. Women of the West African Guinea coast, from Dakar to Yaounde, amaze even the casual visitor with their high degree of emancipation. The contrast with the Muslim societies of the African interior is striking. In Lloyd's (1965) words, "The Yoruba wife's status is characterized by great overt submission to her husband together with considerable economic independence." A man's first marriage typically occurs when he is in the middle to late twenties and when the girl is sixteen to eighteen. The husband makes a series of gifts and payments to the lineage of the bride, and thereby acquires a right to all children born to her during the marriage, to sole sexual access (damages are claimed for adultery), and to his wife's domestic labor. A few years later, the man, if his economic circumstances permit, will try to acquire a second wife, and most men in late middle age are polygynous. Lloyd (1965) estimates that roughly one-third of the men are monogamous, one-third bigamous, and one-third have three or more wives.

The main purpose of marriage is procreation, and the stigma of barrenness for a woman is very strong. Children are highly valued: the more the merrier. On the other hand, divorce is easily obtained and frequent; in one district, 3.5 percent of all extant marriages were broken in any given year, a good proportion of these involving childless women. Little if any stigma is attached to divorce, which is accompanied by repayment to the husband of all or a portion of the bridewealth. After the husband's death, marital rights pass to the deceased's junior brother or son (except, of course, that the son acquires no marital rights over his mother); again, divorce is an easy way out for the woman if she should not be happy with the new arrangement.

A woman's seniority in her husband's compound is determined by her marriage: she is junior to all men born before that time, calls them "husband," and is called "wife" by them. Domestic roles are strictly segregated by sex. Each wife is assigned a separate room in the compound, where she sleeps with her young children; the husband has his own room where the wives take turns visiting him, feeding him, and sleeping with him. Husband and wife do not eat together; the wife serves her husband food on bended knee.

All the foregoing gives the misleading impression that women are completely subordinated to men. The marks of extreme deference which wives lavish on husbands, however, are more an expression of the elaborate Yoruba system of *age* differentiation than an index of the subordination of women; it just happens that, within the household, the husband is always the wife's senior. Besides, as anyone acquainted with Yoruba folk theater well knows, this outward deference etiquette does not preclude women from berating their husbands in the most vituperative language when the occasion arises. The hen-pecked husband is a favorite theme of Yoruba situation comedies.

What, then, makes for the relatively high status of Yoruba women in relation to men? There seem to be two main factors. First, there is a relative absence of a dual standard of sexual morality. Yoruba society is relatively permissive for both men and women; divorce is frequent and about equally easy to obtain for both sexes; and erotic initiative and aggressiveness are not at all male prerogatives.

Next to sexual emancipation, economic independence gives Yoruba women a great deal of power and influence. Retail trading is virtually a female monopoly, and a very high proportion of women do engage in some trading. Surplus foodstuffs, home-woven cloth, and other household products are the woman's to sell for her own profit. She controls her own purse, and, from the profits of trade, she may become completely financially independent of her husband, feeding and dressing herself and her children, and paying the latter's school fees. The more successful female traders are often much richer than their husbands and become true entrepreneurs, investing savings in rental property, in buses, in durable goods stocks, and in similar high-yield activities. The "mammy wagons" of West Africa have become proverbial: these pickup trucks mounted with a wooden body are the main form of long-distance public transport in coastal West Africa, and some women own entire fleets of them. Women traders are organized in extremely effective merchant guilds, monopolizing certain trades (for example, homespun textiles), regulating and policing markets, extending credit, and controlling whole sectors of the traditional economy.

Understandably, the woman's economic leverage translates also into a certain amount of political power and legal rights. For example, both sexes may inherit property from both father and mother, although practices vary in different parts of Yorubaland, and, generally, women's claims to real estate are weaker than men's. A woman retains rights to economic aid, residence, and ritual participation in her own patrilineage after marriage. In a number of Yoruba kingdoms, women were corporately organized in the political field: there was a head woman acting as principal female adviser to the king and presiding over a female council made up of women of wealth, experience, and character. This female council had disciplinary powers over unmarried girls, as well as advisory powers to the king. Although excluded from some important male secret societies and from active participation in certain rituals, women do play an appreciable role in both the political and the economic aspects of public life.

Within the domestic sphere of the extended polygynous family, through seniority, women can acquire considerable power and influence, including over junior males. The senior wife of the head of a *compound* (traditionally, a rectangular set of buildings enclosed in an outer wall with a central patio; this is the abode of the localized segment of the patrilineage) is respectfully addressed as "mistress" of the compound, just as her husband is its "master." And, of course, the successful trader who becomes wealthier than her husband acquires much domestic power and status as well. Even devout Muslim men among the Yoruba do not follow the Islamic practice of keeping their wives in *purdah* (seclusion); in fact, even if they wanted to, the wives would not tolerate it. Through a combination of sexual emancipation, economic independence, seniority, and personal skills, women in Yoruba society, though not the equals of men, come as close to it as they do in any society.

These few illustrations from non-Western societies have not enabled us to cover the range of role variation in the status of women, but they will help us to define the social correlates of sex status. Some of the hypotheses on the subject advanced by earlier generations of anthropologists and still held by laymen have since proved unfounded. It was long believed that matrilineal descent was a residue of matriarchy. In fact, there is no evolutionary evidence that a matriarchal society ever existed, but there is some contemporary evidence that the rule of descent is linked with the status of women. Matrilineal societies are also male dominated, but on the whole less so than patrilineal ones. In both cases, authority is passed on *between males*, but, in patrilineal societies, the transmission takes place directly from brother to brother and from father to son, while in matrilineal societies, authority is passed *through* a woman, namely from mother's brother to mother's son.

In the three examples we examined, the status of women is lowest among the Hausa, who have bilateral descent, highest among the patrilineal Yoruba, and fairly high among the double descent Tuareg. The case is thus inconclusive. Reanalyzing Simmons' (1945) sample of seventy-one societies, Gouldner and Peterson (1962) report that inferiority of women is correlated +.44 with patrilineal descent and -.34 with matrilineal descent, accounting for respectively 19 percent and 15 percent of the variance. The relationship is definitely significant, but the sample of societies is relatively small and not random. More closely related to the status of women than the rule of descent, however, were inheritance of property and succession of authority. Patrilineal property inheritance is correlated +.58 with the subjection of women, and patrilineal authority succession, +.51. Thus, the role played by women in the devolution of power and property, whether in the women's own right or as necessary genealogical links, seems to be a better predictor of female status in relation to men than filiation as such. Not surprisingly, control of power and wealth determines status more than anything else.

There is evidence that rule of residence has some bearing on the status of women, though the relationship, if it exists, is not strong. It seems that women are in a better position with men in uxorilocal and neolocal societies than in virilocal ones. As any normally neolocal Westerner visiting in-laws quickly realizes, the spouse who is on home ground has a certain advantage over the one who is away from home. Neolocality neutralizes that effect, and where it is the rule, any departure from it causes marital tensions, in good part because it disturbs the balance of power between spouses. A woman who spends all her life among her own kinsmen is in a better position relative to her husband than one who must live with her husband's relatives. Even in the fairly rare (about 15 percent of the Murdock sample) case of uxorilocal residence, however, it does not follow that the woman is in a more advantageous position with her male relatives who wield the power; it simply means that in the typical uxorilocal, matrilineal society, women are under the authority of their brothers or matrilateral uncles rather than that of their husbands or husband's fathers. Since all three of the examples we examined are virilocal, as indeed are some two-thirds of the world's societies, they do not shed any light on this hypothesis. Gouldner and Peterson (1962) report a low correlation (.25) between subjection of women and virilocal versus uxorilocal residence, supporting the hypothesis but accounting for only 6 percent of the variance.

The form of marriage is often thought to be related to the status of women, polygyny being associated with relatively low status, and monogamy or polyandry with high status. Cross-cultural evidence does not clearly support that hypothesis. Polyandry is a very uncommon arrangement. It makes up only 0.7 percent of Murdock's World Ethnographic Sample of 565 societies (Murdock, 1957). Where it occurs, the upper class males are polygynous, choosing wives not only from their own class but also from strata below them; this produces a general "suction" of women toward the top of the class hierarchy, and leaves lower status males the alternative of celibacy or polyandry. Sometimes, also, polyandry is a correlate of female infanticide, as among the Eskimos. In any case, the arrangement is not an index of the power of women. Monogamy is indeed the lot of the majority of married men in most societies, even in those that allow polygyny. The approximately equal sex ratio insures that. However, the great majority of the world's societies (75.6 percent in Murdock's sample) have not only allowed polygyny, but made it the *preferred* form of marriage. The societies in which polygyny is proscribed, though numerically large and on the whole in the ascendancy, are in terms of total number of societies (23.7 percent of Murdock's sample) very much in the minority. With urbanization and industrialization, the Western practice of monogamy is slowly spreading to some non-Western societies, but not nearly as fast as might be supposed. For example, in much of Africa, among Christians and Muslims alike, polygyny is still tenaciously preferred, at least by men, and not infrequently by women as well.

Since a great deal of ethnocentric and moralistic nonsense has been spoken about polygyny, let us define briefly the conditions under which it occurs. There are basically two types of polygyny, usually referred to as *harem* and *hut*. *Harem polygyny*, as typified by the traditional Muslim Arab and Persian societies, is characterized by the seclusion of women in segregated common quarters, often under the guard of eunuchs. Popularized in the West through comic operas and legends such as the *Arabian Nights*, the harem became accepted as the prototype of polygyny, whereas, in fact, it is a very special case. Under harem polygyny, the status of women is indeed low. Of course, even within those societies, the harem is a privilege enjoyed only by the ruler and the nobility, and is thus not a generalized practice.

Far more common is *hut polygyny*, so called because each wife has a separate dwelling. Since the type is so prevalent in Africa, and since Europeans have insisted on calling African houses "huts," the institution has become known as *hut polygyny*. Under that system, each wife and her children constitute a semiautonomous subfamily, typically with separate sleeping and cooking quarters, and often with separate means of economic sustenance as well (market stall, land, and so on). The polygynous household then becomes not a herd of women at the lascivious whim of their lord and master, but rather a set of small economic and child-raising groups tied together through a common husband and father. Almost invariably, there are norms against favoritism on the part of the husband, and rotation roles determining when the various wives are to sleep with and cook for their common husband. Also, there is nearly always an order of seniority establishing a scale of prestige and authority among wives, and other mechanisms to regulate cowife rivalry and jealousy. What the older wives may lose in sexual attractiveness and child-bearing ability, they gain in status, wealth, and power.

A common question concerning polygyny is how, given a nearly equal sex ratio, it is possible to maintain a substantial incidence of plural marriages without condemning some men to celibacy. The answer is quite simple: by maintaining a large age difference between husbands and wives. Typically, the system works as follows: on first marriage, the bride is in her teens and the groom in his mid- to late twenties; a few years later, when the man has accumulated sufficient wealth to pay for the bridewealth of a second wife, and when his increased social status makes polygyny a social "must," he will marry a second wife who may be as much as twenty years his junior;

another decade or so later he might marry a third wife who is even younger. Upon his death, his surviving widows, some of them still quite young, remarry, often according to well-defined rules of "widow inheritance" among brothers or between father and son. Thus, women enter the marital circuit much younger, and often go through several husbands in temporal sequence, whereas husbands have several wives simultaneously. The extent to which men are polygynous is closely related to the age of the man and to his wealth. Polygynous husbands are older men of substance; thus, it follows that polygyny becomes a symbol of status for both husband and wife. The larger the mean age difference in favor of husbands, the more polygyny is possible, making it feasible for most men of advanced middle age to be small-scale polygynists (two to four wives), and for most women to be married to a polygynist for at least part of their lifetime.

Two other misconceptions concerning polygyny have led to the Western assumption that polygyny is demeaning to women. The first is that the man's principal motivation for polygyny is sexual. Naturally, sexual attraction may be a contributing factor to a man's seeking another wife, but it is only one of several reasons. A man's incentives for polygyny are typically a combination of status drive, the desire for more numerous progeny (especially in a patrilineal system in which the size of the lineage is a direct function of the number of wives), a search for ritual security (that is, having many sons to carry on the ancestor cult), a drive for political power through the multiplication of ties with well-placed in-laws, and a means of accumulating wealth, where women play an important part in the productive process. If one's second or third wife also happens to be a comely young lady, all the better, but sexual motivation in marriage is seldom as prominent in polygynous societies as it is in Western monogamous societies.

From a young woman's perspective, if the choice is (as it often boils down to) between becoming the overworked single wife of a struggling young man or a spoiled junior wife in the large and respected household of a middle-aged man of substance and wealth, the preference is not all that obvious, especially as she is not expected to marry for love in either case. In many polygynous societies, the choice of junior wives depends in part on the consent of the senior wife whose own status, both within and outside the household, is enhanced when her husband becomes a polygynist. With European contact and the influence of Christian missionaries, Western-educated African women have often adopted the European denigration of polygyny. However, the evidence simply does not allow one to conclude that polygyny depresses the status of women allegedly because it reduces them to sexual objects at the mercy of lascivious old men. Magazines and television commercials in monogamous

America are much more demeaning to women than any institution that might be found in the average polygynous society.

Frequently, in the micropolitics of the polygynous household, cowives ally themselves against the husband (for example, to extort gifts), who has a hard time holding his own. In fact, it might be plausibly argued that monogamy is the most politically atomizing form of marriage for women, while polygyny favors the development of sex solidarity. In practice, of course, cowifehood is both a divisive and a cohesive force from the woman's perspective. One thing is certain—polygyny does not, except in the "harem" form, work systematically to the detriment of women. Two of the societies we examined were polygynous: in one, the status of women was very low; in the other, it was certainly higher than in many monogamous societies.

The second prevalent misconception concerning marriage in polygynous societies results from the mercenary interpretation applied to the institution of *brideprice* or *bridewealth*. These terms, because they emphasize the monetary aspect of the institution, are misleading. *Dowry* would be a much better term, even though in the Western tradition it refers to the wife's bringing a material consideration into the marriage rather than the far more common opposite arrangement. In most polygynous societies, the groom's family makes a series of ritualized gifts, sometimes of considerable material value, to the kin group of the bride. Far from being a quasi-commercial transaction akin to slavery, wherein women are bartered against livestock, the dowry or bridewealth is in fact the guarantee of the legality of the marriage and of the legitimacy of the future offspring. It is part of the ritual that makes the marriage binding. The fact that in cases of the woman's barrenness, the bridewealth is often returned, shows that the stress is put at least as much on parental rights over the offspring as on marital rights over the wife. The dowry not only does not reduce the woman to the status of chattel; it frequently serves as a warranty for the good behavior of the husband and a factor in marriage stability.[7]

A prominent Marxist theory on the status of women (first extensively developed by Friedrich Engels) links their subordination to their lack of a productive role in society. According to that theory, the subordination of women is a direct function

---

[7]With Western contact, the dowry in some Africal societies began to be paid in cash as distinguished from livestock and other traditional media. As a consequence of urban conditions, missionary derogation of the institution, and other factors, the bridewealth began to change its meaning and functions and to acquire a more mercenary character. This, however, represents a perversion of its traditional meaning.

of their being debarred from making a significant contribution to the productive process, and of their being kept in the domestic sphere as mere consumers or, at best, transformers of goods produced by men. As applied to industrial societies, the reason that women are treated as inferiors is that, in a capitalistic, materialistic system, money is the measure of all things. Since many women spend much of their time in unpaid household tasks, the product of their labor, and hence their very persons, are devalued.

Washburn and De Vore (1961a) propose a more speculative evolutionary theory that links male dominance both with the emergence of the human family and with the system of production. They argue rather convincingly that sometime during the Middle Pleistocene epoch (approximately one million years ago) the human family began to emerge as a social adaptation for the purpose of hunting large animals. This subsistence activity put a premium on cooperation among men and on exogamous mating. Hunting large mammals over vast territories gave men a substantial productive advantage over women and increased the dependence of women and children.

There is, of course, a precise opposite to the Marxist theory of female subordination, namely, that in those societies in which women do the bulk of the onerous productive labor, as they do in a good many African agricultural societies, they are being exploited by men as beasts of burden. The empirical truth of the matter is that there seems to be no simple relationship between the status of women and their role in the productive process. If productive behavior were automatically ennobling, slaves would become kings. A correlation (whether as cause, as effect, or both) does seem to exist between the amount of control women have over *property* and its inheritance and their status in relation to men. What seems to be rewarded and rewarding, then, is not the productivity of one's toil, but the control of wealth, whatever its source might be (Gouldner & Peterson, 1962).[8]

Finally, there is a theory that technology is the great emancipator of women. In its naïve, commercialized form, the theory becomes the Madison Avenue slogan pushing the latest mechanical contrivance to "free" the suburban housewife from the drudgery of housework. In its more sophisticated form, the argument runs that, since the only thing in which women might be

---

[8] If there is any relationship between the importance of the contribution of women in productive labor and anything else, it is with war. The more time men spend killing each other, the more subsistence work falls to the women, at least in those agricultural societies in which warfare would interfere with productive work if it were done primarily by men (Ember, 1971).

admitted to be inferior to men is brute strength, and since technology makes sheer muscle power increasingly obsolete, advanced technology acts as a sex equalizer and destroys the last semblance of legitimacy for male supremacist ideology.

Empirical evidence seems to give only partial confirmation to this theory. The relationship between technology and the status of women appears to be curvilinear. By and large (and with a good many exceptions), the status of women is relatively lowest in the advanced agrarian societies, such as preindustrial Europe, Asia, and the Near East. Conversely, woman's status is relatively highest in the technologically simplest societies, especially the hunting and gathering ones. The Pygmies of the Congo rain forest, for example, are as nearly egalitarian in all respects including sex, as in any human society (Turnbull, 1961, 1965). With the industrialization of agrarian societies, however, women have generally gained in status relative to the nadir of their position in the preindustrial era, but as we shall see in Chapter 7, industrial societies are still far from being sex egalitarian. The relationship between technology and sex status is neither simple nor direct. An advanced technology may enhance the possibility of sex equality, but it does not by any means insure its actuality.

We must close this chapter, therefore, with the dissatisfying admission that we are still far from having an accurate picture of what determines the relative status of men and women. We have suggested a few gross structural relationships, discarded a few erroneous notions, and gained some perspective on the range of variability and uniformity in sex differentiation across human societies. Now we must try to do the same for age differentiation.

5 Age Differentiation in Human Societies

Because age differences are biologically based, they are recognized in all human societies. There is not only an obvious cognitive awareness of age and aging, but there are also social differences linked with role expectations and status. That is, age is *put to social use* in creating differentiated social structures. The biological constraints of age are obvious and are, of course, reflected in social structure: a two-year-old and an eighty-year-old would both make poor warriors or wet nurses. There are age constraints also on the physiological maturity necessary for an infant to learn to walk, talk, and acquire other skills basic to all societies. Even as late as puberty, there might be a biological basis to the acquisition or nonacquisition of cultural skills. For example, until puberty, the majority of people are able to learn to speak new languages without noticeable foreign accents, whereas after puberty, full phonetic mastery is exceptional (Lenneberg, 1967).

However, the social use of age extends well beyond these obvious constraints. In all societies, birth, puberty, and death are important social events marked by *rites of passage*. Infants are given few responsibilities, but gradually they are trained, consciously and unconsciously, to behave according to their particular position in society (especially, according to their age and sex roles). As the infant becomes a young child —a stage achieved in most societies when the child is fully mobile, weaned, toilet trained, and perhaps most importantly, when he has mastered his language well enough to communicate with other members of his society—he is initiated into social responsibilities commensurate with his skills and strength.[1]

---

[1] With the full realization that English syntax (and that of many other languages besides) reflects the male bias of the

At or near puberty, a ritual typically marks the social recognition of adult status, which means reasonableness and responsibility. Often, this recognition precedes by a few years marriageability or full civic status. Young adulthood is devoted to economic production, warfare, and procreating and nurturing infants. For some males, older adulthood is a time for political leadership. Even death does not put an individual's social role to an end: through some conception of immortality, he becomes a silent partner in a continuing ritual relationship.

Beyond the broad similarities in the social recognition of maturation and aging, including the attendant abilities and disabilities, the plasticity of human behavior is wide, unlike that of any other animal. One variable is the relative importance of age compared to other aspects of social differentiation. Naturally, this is inversely related to the total degree of differentiation in a given society. In many of the "simpler" societies, social organization is nearly defined by the types of differentiated relationships based respectively on kinship, marriage, age, and sex. Any one of these necessarily looms large, but even among these societies there is a considerable range in the importance of age. In the more complexly differentiated societies, especially in industrial societies, age loses in relative importance partly because there are more competing bases of social organization, such as class, ethnicity, religion, occupation, voluntary associations, and the like, and partly because technology emancipates man from age-specific disabilities.

A second important age-linked variable is the degree to which, in a given society, age forms the basis of a corporate social grouping. To be sure, in all societies, age labels are used to refer to such broad social categories as "children," "young men," or "the elders." But, societies differ widely depending on whether age labels refer to ill-defined aggregates of people covering a wide age span (for example, terms such as *senior citizen* or *my generation* in American society) or to a self-conscious, precisely-defined group of close coevals (for example, "the Harvard Class of 1970"). Some societies, especially in Africa, stress heavily the importance of the latter type of age grouping. For these precisely-defined, self-conscious, corporate age groups, we shall use the terms *age grades* and *age sets*. The former term we shall use when the emphasis is on the position of that age category in relation to similar others, for example, "The sophomore class at Harvard"

---

society that produced it, I shall nevertheless continue to use masculine pronouns to refer to members of both sexes until such time as we manage to get new ones accepted into standard English.

is in our terms an *age grade*. We shall reserve the term *age set* for the specific group of individuals who move up as a group through an age grade system. For example, "the Harvard class of 1970" is an age *set* until its last member dies; in 1966, it entered the freshman age *grade*, in 1967, the sophomore one, and so on, until, in 1970, its successful members superannuated themselves out of the four-grade system and became life-long elders or *alumni*. Entire societies are principally organized around such age sets and age grades, as we shall see.

A third dimension of age differentiation is the stress put on *relative versus absolute age*. Is the sociologically important question that A is 55 years old and B, 67, or simply that B is A's senior? In Western societies, an unusual stress is put on absolute age, a concomitant of an almost compulsively elaborate and precise system of timekeeping. There are relatively few societies in which being born on April 15, 1945, for example, is a matter of any social consequence. In fact, many societies manage quite happily not keeping track at all of the year, much less the month and day of birth of their members. In those societies, the sociologically important fact is *relative seniority*. Nor must it be thought, as ethnocentric Westerners often have, that lack of concern for one's absolute age is merely a reflection of ignorance or of the society's inability to keep a calendar. In many traditional societies of Africa, for example, in which people do not "know their age," they time their agricultural activities precisely according to a lunar calendar.

At the other end of the spectrum, we find Western societies in which a person's birthday is, next to his name, the most socially important fact concerning him—a fact that needs to be officially certified, failing which he will have difficulty in enrolling in a school, obtaining a passport to travel abroad, getting married, obtaining a driver's license, purchasing liquor, qualifying for retirement, and so on. Western man is almost unthinkable without a birth certificate. As might be expected, the consequences of European countries trying to enforce on African societies an absolute conception of age and a mania for timekeeping have often been ludicrous. Some African bureaucracies have taken over from their former colonial masters the worship of the birth certificate, and people simply choose a date of birth at random within the plausible range. The only limitation is that once you have chosen an age, you have to stick with it. The state has learned to accept one fictional date of birth per person, but it still balks at two.

Relative age is of far more widespread significance. Indeed, it is of some importance in all cultures, and of paramount consequence in a good many. Perhaps one of the most widespread and general concepts of relative age is *generation*, which links age to the kinship system, both laterally and linearly. In systems of bilateral descent, in which lineages and clans are absent, such as in Western societies, the concept of generation has been extended to mean one's approximate coevals, the narrowness of the age limits varying according to the circumstances. Thus, a "student generation" at a university covers roughly four or five years, that is, the people who were there synchronously with ego. In the broader societal context, a generation spans twenty to twenty-five years, but since the reference is to an ego placed in the middle of that span, it means, in effect, people born within ten or twelve years of ego, that is, those not old enough to be ego's parents nor young enough to be his children.

In the far more common type of society characterized by unilineal descent, whether matrilineal or patrilineal, the concept of generation becomes more specific. Where there are clearly defined lineages and clans, it becomes possible to order all of one's relatives by generation in relation to oneself. Thus, in one's parental generation belong his parents, his grandparents' children, his great-grandparents' children's children, and so on. Often, the same kin term may be used for father and father's brother, or for mother and mother's sister, or for brother and father's brother's son. Naturally, when the concept of generation is so closely linked to kin ties, it correlates less closely with age—over three generations, and especially with a polygynous system, there is typically some overlap in age between a man's younger children and his older grandchildren.

This leads us to the distinction between what we may call *sociological versus chronological age*. If the generational criterion of seniority is paramount, then it may happen that the chronological junior becomes the sociological senior, for example, the junior uncle outranks the senior nephew. The same situation can also arise in age-grade systems in which there is often some overlap in chronological age between sets. Some college sophomores are younger than some freshmen, yet, sociologically, in the college age-grade system, sophomores are sociologically senior to freshmen, irrespective of birth order. Seniority is relative, but in this case, not to individuals' birth order, a mere biological accident in this context; rather, it is relative to two *groups* in an age-hierarchized system.

An extremely important aspect of age differentiation is hierarchy. Age is almost by definition a hierarchical criterion causing *asymmetrical relations*, at least between adults and children. All societies are ruled by adults, despite the observation that the behavior of American children sometimes gives the impression that the United States is an exception to the rule. However, societies vary considerably in the extent to which age is a pervasive and significant criterion of hierarchy outside the family, schools, and other child socialization agencies. Some societies are relatively egalitarian on the age dimension, whereas, in others, age is the paramount criterion of differentiation in power, wealth, status, inheritance, and other scarce resources.

By and large, age stratification seems most pronounced in those societies in which other bases of invidious status distinction (class, caste, race, ethnicity) are absent or undeveloped. Conversely, Western industrial societies are less prominently age-stratified and have become decreasingly so over time, except for their educational systems, which are rigidly stratified and segregated by age. Privileges of primogeniture, once so important in several parts of Europe in preventing the breakup of landed estates and the outbreak of fratricidal civil wars, whenever the throne became vacant, are only vestigial today (mainly, in the inheritance of the crown in the few remaining constitutional monarchies). Rank, of course, is correlated with age and "seniority" in most modern bureaucracies, but other criteria take precedence. Typically, modern bureaucracies are stratified into two or three educational and class levels (officers versus noncommissioned ranks in the army, for example), so that the lower ranks of the upper stratum are much younger than the upper ranks of the lower group.

In most Western societies, parents lose legal rights and responsibilities over their children at age twenty-one, and there is a tendency toward lowering the age of political and legal responsibility to eighteen. There are still some vestiges of age deference in forms of speech and etiquette, but status, power, and income drop sharply after retirement age (usually sixty to sixty-five for men, and even earlier for women). Allowing for differences from occupation to occupation, positions of greatest power and wealth are typically held by men in their late forties, fifties, or early sixties, but such hierarchy as exists is only incidentally correlated, rather than causally linked, with age. Promotion by seniority is seldom the paramount principle, and, even then, years of service matter more than chronological age.

In European languages that differentiate between a "polite" and a "familiar" form (for example, French: *tu-vous*; German: *Du-Sie*; and Spanish: *tu-usted*), the forms are often used asymmetrically between adults and children who are unrelated to each other, but reciprocally between parents and children. Furthermore, the etiquette across age lines often applies across class lines as well, and class etiquette may even supersede age etiquette. Thus, as we see in nineteenth-century European novels, a social superior may address his chronologically senior subordinate in the familiar form, and expect him to reply in the polite form.

Another negative correlate of age stratification is associated with the rate of change, especially technological change.

The increasingly rapid obsolescence of skills makes it difficult for older workers to vindicate their claims to higher status in an industrial economy that stresses productivity and efficiency (whether under capitalism or socialism). Beyond the "prime of life"—the thirties for women, the forties for men—increasing age is, by and large a social liability in Western societies. To some extent, the professional elite is shielded from the adverse effects of advancing age, but, for the majority, the advantages of growing old are few. Although by no means all older people are poor, for example, the aged, along with the blacks, are among the most impoverished strata of the American population.

In the sphere of kinship, also, the principle of seniority plays a minimal role in Western societies. In the absence of any large corporate kin units, such as lineages and clans, seniority does not have any collateral extension: older siblings have little authority over their younger brothers and sisters, much less over younger siblings' children. Parents can, with mixed success, impose their will upon their minor children, but any legal authority is extinguished when children reach twenty-one. Grandparents exercise only limited authority over grandchildren, and then, largely *in loco parentis*. In short, since the nuclear family is by far the most meaningful kinship group in industrialized Western societies, it is not surprising that seniority in the kinship system operates almost solely within the nuclear family, and only until children reach adult status. Even within the nuclear family, there is a clear tendency, at least in the urbanized middle classes, toward more age-egalitarian relationships.

The contrast in age stratification with most nonindustrial, non-Western societies is striking. The prototypical social organization of a great many non-Western societies is the local unilineal descent group, including the in-marrying spouses from other lineages and clans. For the sake of illustration, let us take a common form of kinship organization in nonindustrial societies—the extended, polygynous, virilocal family with exogamous clans and lineages based on patrilineal descent. Under such a system, all the descendants of a putative ancestor form a clan, itself subdivided into lineages of varying generational depth, descent being traced only in the single male line. The male members of a lineage or segment thereof live in physical proximity to each other, together with the unmarried female members of the lineage, and with wives who have come from other lineages. The residential kin group is an extended family spanning three or four generations, and including collateral branches. As such systems are frequently polygynous, these localized lineages may include hundreds of persons.

With few exceptions, and with provisions made for senility and other forms of mental incapacity, the authority structure of such large kin groups is based on seniority, the simplest and most universal way of solving the authority problem with a minimum of contention and argument. Authority passes from father to oldest son, then through the line of sons until the last member of the generation dies, then to the oldest son of the oldest son, and so on. There are, of course, numerous variants on this basic pattern, and localized lineages typically break up. The segments establish a new residence as the group becomes too large, or as conflict develops between brothers and half-brothers after the death of their father. In principle, however, the oldest male in the lineage holds legal authority over all members of the lineage, including the descendants of his brothers and brothers' sons.

The seniority principle is typically symbolized (as are other forms of inequality) through a distinct etiquette regulating formal interaction between age unequals. Among the Yoruba of southwestern Nigeria, for example, who, in common with many other African peoples, have an elaborate age deference etiquette, the language prescribes two forms of address, one familiar, one deferential, which are used nonreciprocally between juniors and seniors, and even between siblings who are no more than a year apart. Furthermore, the junior upon meeting a senior must prostrate himself to the ground if male, and kneel with bowed head if female. In the contemporary urban context, these age deference patterns become somewhat attenuated, but the principle is still powerful enough to create acutely embarrassing situations when it comes into conflict with other nontraditional forms of inequality. Thus, relations between master and servant, or between superior and subordinate in the civil service become tense if the person superior in class or rank is junior in age. Frequently, such situations are either avoided altogether (for example, by not hiring a domestic servant who is one's senior), or various evasive techniques are used to minimize the embarrassment, such as speaking English to sidestep the Yoruba spoken age deference.

In a number of societies, the seniority principle among siblings, so crucial in establishing lines of succession and authority in kin groups, is entrenched in the kinship terminology. There may be, for example, two entirely different kin terms to designate "junior brother" and "senior brother," as among some Maya languages. This senior-junior brother relationship may be considered so basic that its absence is inconceivable. Once, as I was doing field work in the Chiapas highlands of southeastern Mexico, a Maya area in which religion is a combination of Catholicism and indigenous beliefs, I noticed a statue of the Virgin Mary, but she had two children on her lap, one larger than the other. When I asked a Maya Indian for an explanation, he told me that one infant was "Jesus-older-brother" and the other "Jesus-younger-brother."

Since authority is mainly exercised by men, seniority is generally more developed among males; it is not, however, restricted to them. In many polygynous societies, the principle of seniority among wives of the same husband is resorted to, in order to reduce conflict among them. Typically, the first wife is senior over the others and exercises a measure of authority over them. The first wife is nearly always the oldest, since polygyny is normally serial (a man marries his first wife when he is twenty-five, his second one ten or twelve years later, and there is a steeply increasing age disparity between husband and wife with each successive marriage).

In most societies, even the relatively undifferentiated ones, ties of solidarity link kin groups together into larger political units. A common arrangement is one in which the lineage heads (determined by seniority within the descent group) collectively constitute a "council of elders." This may take the form of a decentralized village political structure, in which the elders, acting as a body, exercise judicial, executive, and legislative functions. Or, such a council of elders may act as a representative body of their respective kin groups to a centralized authority. Often, the elders function as a body of councilors to the king, representing the mass of commoners. The elders are ineligible for the kingship, but they are not uncommonly the kingmakers, choosing the sovereign from the eligible princes in the royal clan. Thus, within unilineal descent groups, a seniority principle for the transmission and legitimation of authority may become generalized and furnish the basis of political integration for societies of hundreds of thousands of people.

Another interesting generalization of the principle of seniority occurs when the concept of age ranking is extended from individuals to groups. It is one thing to say that A is senior to his brother B, and thus has authority over B and his children so long as A lives. When A dies, B then assumes authority over A's children, and no segment of the lineage is permanently under the authority of someone who is not a direct ascendant. It is quite another thing, however, to claim that because A is senior to his brother B, his *segment of the lineage* has collective authority over B's. Such a claim, that a whole branch is senior to the others, establishes a permanent hierarchy among *groups of people*. Yet, ethnographic evidence suggests that such a claim has frequently been made, and, along with military conquest, constitutes perhaps one of the two most common ways of establishing in one stroke a system of centralized government and a genuine class system. In effect, when such a claim of collective seniority is successfully made (that is, when the claim becomes accepted by "junior" descent groups), the "senior" group has the potential of turning itself into a ruling aristocracy. The senior group becomes a royal clan from which the king is chosen, and the other clans or lineages are reduced to the status of commoners. A number of centralized African kingdoms may have developed out of what anthropologists call *acephalous* or *segmentary lineage* societies in the way just sketched. What were originally societies segmented into unranked unilineal descent groups and devoid of centralized authority (that is, stateless) may have grown into stratified, politically centralized states through a seniority claim of one of its component lineages or clans.

Interestingly, within the royal clan of many African kingdoms, there is no rule of primogeniture. Quite often, *any* son of the previous king is eligible. Combined with extensive royal polygyny, this rule frequently creates a class of several scores or even hundreds of eligible princes. Not uncommonly, the choice from among the potential claimants is made by a council of elders drawn by seniority from commoner lineages.

The concept of *group seniority* may operate within an aristocracy also, as it did in Europe, where primogeniture was well established. A king or nobleman could pass on his title only to his first son, his younger sons receiving a title one rung lower in the noble hierarchy. Thus, the brothers of a reigning king would be princes or grand dukes, and the younger brothers of a duke would be earls or marquis. Descendants of several brothers would be referred to as the "senior" or "junior" branches of the family, even though European societies had already moved away from unilateral to bilateral descent.

So far, in dealing with age in nonindustrial and non-Western societies, we have stressed its linkages with the family and the kinship system. Perhaps the most creative and extensive use of age as a criterion for social differentiation, however, has been achieved by *emancipating* age from kinship. The principle of age sets and age grades is not unique to Africa; it has had some limited applications in other societies, as illustrated by our Western age-graded educational system. However, an age-grade system as a primary basis of society-wide integration is indeed characteristic of Africa. This is not to say that all African societies have age grades, nor even that most of them attribute age grades overwhelming importance. Within Africa, the functions and importance attributed to age grades and age sets vary greatly (Eisenstadt, 1956, 1965). But, the "classical" age-grade societies of East Africa such as the Nandi, Kipsigi, Masai, Kamba, Kikuyu, Meru, and others are uniquely African. Even though the details of the system vary among these, a general pattern clearly emerges.

In summary, the system works as follows. Every few years, a group of boys born within a few years of each other are initiated together into adult society, thereby bringing into existence a new age set occupying the most junior age-grade position. That age set, usually named, remains in existence until its last member dies. After the period of initiation, the age set is typically closed, and no initiations take place for a few years, until a new batch of initiates forms the next age set. When that happens, all previous age sets move up by one age grade. That is, the creation of a new age set through initiation of the next group of boys is the signal for a massive promotion exercise in which all previous age sets assume the age grade position hitherto occupied by their immediately senior age set.

The time interval between age sets varies from society to society, typically ranging from seven to fifteen years; the number of age sets in existence at a given time varies also. The functions of age sets differ, ranging from recreational clubs to the basis of military organization and government. In some societies, each age set enjoys a great deal of autonomy (freedom from control from seniors), whereas in others, this autonomy is much more restricted. Overriding these differences, however, age-set systems exhibit common characteristics: they cut across kin groups; they establish society-wide ties of solidarity among coevals; and, they establish a stratification that, though resulting in the differential distribution of status and power, is nevertheless democratic and universal for men. In short, age sets both stratify and integrate societies on a basis other than kinship, and in a way that, for men, is as uninvidious as possible. Every boy gets initiated, and, once in the system, a man need only survive to be promoted.

Let us look more closely at a stateless society like the Masai, in which age sets are maximally important. The Masai are a pastoralist, seminomadic people, numbering around 300,000, and occupying a vast area of southern Kenya and northern Tanzania, which they conquered in a series of military raids in the late nineteenth century, just before the British and German conquests. They herd cattle, sheep, and goats, and use donkeys as beasts of burden, but engage in no agriculture, and despise their peasant neighbors. Their diet consists mostly of the meat, milk, and blood of their herds. Slaughtering cattle is uncommon and done mostly on ritual occasions, but cows are milked, and the Masai, like many other African pastoralists, periodically bleed their cattle by carefully puncturing a neck vein. Cattle are not simply an economic asset, but also a social one, being essential in the payment of the bridewealth, without which no marriage or parenthood is legal. Like most African peoples, the Masai are patrilineal and their kinship system is organized on the basis of the extended, polygynous, virilocal family. The Masai have lineages and clans, but these kin groups do not have the overwhelming importance that they assume in a number of stateless societies, such as the Nuer, in which they constitute the principal social organization.

Unlike the many politically centralized societies of Africa, the Masai have no state, in the sense of clearly distinct political institutions (like a bureaucracy, a police force, tax-collecting machinery, tribunals) and a group of officials (king, ministers, army officers, spies, judges, executioners) specializing in wielding power over their fellow men. As do all societies, the Masai have a government—that is, a system of rules of conduct to regulate internal conflict and maintain internal peace. The term *acephalous* applied to stateless societies, in which power is diffuse and there is no king or chief, is misleading, for such societies are anything but "headless" or anarchical. They are rather polycephalous, that is, ruled collectively by councils of elders, often with a considerable measure of democracy for adult men.

The Masai, in common with many other East African pastoralists, and indeed some agriculturalists as well, have made age the paramount principle of social integration, ritual activity, government, and military organization. Prior to the "pacification" imposed by the European conquest, these societies were extremely bellicose; they were efficiently organized as permanent cattle-raiding machines that had universal military service for young adult men. The Masai, whose spectacular military successes against the Kikuyu and other groups have become a legend and an East African embodiment of the romantic Noble Savage theme, have been extensively studied by anthropologists. Bernardi (1955) gives us the best and most extensive account of their age-set system.

Around adolescence, boys undergo a long series of initiation rituals, during which they are segregated from the rest of the society for several months, are circumcised, have their heads shaved by their mother, and are presented by their father with a spear, sword, and shield, the weapons of the Masai warrior. After circumcision, boys are said to have "become men," but, in fact, they are still several years away from full adult status. They are not allowed to marry or own cattle, they are subjected to food taboos, and they are under the supervision of elders. Boys are initiated during the rainy season, a time of abundance, and initiations take place in cycles of roughly four successive years. Starting at time X, the boys initiated during the time interval of $X + 4$ years are referred to as the "right-hand circumcision" and become the senior subset within the age grade of warriors. For the time being, they are still regarded as apprentices, and, though allowed to take part in raids, they are expected to accompany more senior warriors. The batch of boys initiated during a single rainy season constitutes a subdivision within that four-year subset, but these smaller groupings are of minor significance, though they do establish an order of seniority within the subset.

After usually four years, the subset is closed and no initiations take place for three years or so. Then, at time $X + 7$ years, initiations start anew, and a second subset is opened, referred to as "left-hand circumcision." By this time, the older warriors in the senior subset assume their full status as senior warriors, and the new initiates make up the junior subset between the times of $X+7$ and $X+11$ years. Then, again the subset is closed for about three years, until time $X+15$ years, when the total age set is promoted, and a new set is opened, repeating the fifteen-year cycle.

Thus, all the young men initiated between times X and $X+15$ years make up the age grade of warriors on active duty, internally subdivided into a senior and a junior subgrade. The young men range in age from around fourteen to thirty. A pattern of rivalry, including mock combat, exists between the senior and the junior subsets, sometimes resulting in wounds. These conflicts, far from being condemned, are looked upon with favor.

The entire age set of warriors, made up of unmarried men, remains under the supervision of a special group of senior elders known as *piron*, who control and perform the initiation ceremonies, institute the new age sets, assist the initiates, and sponsor them. The warriors live in segregated villages, known as *manyatta*, where food is cooked by their mothers, and where young girls are present for their sexual diversion.[2]

---

[2]Residential segregation by age is by no means unique to the Masai, nor even to stateless, pastoralist societies. For example, the Nyakyusa of southern Tanzania (described by Wilson, 1951) are an agricultural society organized in small chieftainships. There, groups of coevals establish separate residence for the duration of their lifetimes. There results a pattern of quasi-neolocal residence and nuclear (but polygynous) families, very uncommon in Africa. Adolescent boys leave their parents to establish age villages, where their wives will later join them. Unlike the far more common African arrangement of the extended virilocal family, in which three or four generations of the male descendants of a man and their wives share a common residence, the Nyakyusa are sharply segregated by generation. As Wilson (1951, pp. 31-32) describes the arrangement: "There are always villages of three generations in existence— those of contemporaries of the late chief, the headmen of which have ritual functions; those of mature men, contemporaries of the ruling chief, whose headmen have administration and military functions; and those of boys and young men, contemporaries of the heir, who have not yet 'come out' and who fight under the leadership of their fathers' senior headman. . . . Each age-grade, or generation, covers a span of 5 to 8 years." As in most societies, the ruling generation are the men in mature middle age (roughly between thirty-five and sixty-five), and not the oldest. Among the Nyakyusa, as among the Masai and

They are, however, strictly forbidden to marry and own cattle, and are still economically under the control of their fathers, who own the cattle necessary for bridewealth payment, and socially under the collective control of the senior elders. When a subset of "right-hand circumcision" warriors accedes to senior warrior status through the opening of a "left-hand circumcision" subset below them, a ceremony takes place and a leader of the subset is chosen by consultation between the elders and the members of the subset. That post, though highly honored, is not considered as desirable because the leader or *aunoni* is expected to start behaving as an elder, and to marry and settle down before his time. The *aunoni* is a link between the warriors and the elders, being granted elder status despite his membership in the warrior age grade. He is obeyed by his age mates, but he is, in fact, under the control of the *piron* elders, and is not in any strict sense an executive head. There are other officers of the age set, but these too have ritual and honorific rather than executive functions, and the age set is an internally egalitarian institution despite finer age gradings within it. Within the age set there is a small group of opinion leaders and decision makers, often made up of the older members of the set, but also open to individual skills. These leaders have very limited freedom of action, and they can be demoted by a council of their age mates.

The group of young men living in a given warrior village or *manyatta* constitutes a *sirit* of fifty to one hundred people. Common residence establishes a close bond among age mates, and is also the foundation of military organization. Members of a *sirit* fight shoulder to shoulder. Thus, there are two main principles of age-set solidarity: contemporaneity of initiation and commonality of residence in the *manyatta*. This powerful solidarity is reflected in several aspects of life besides military organization. Members of the same age set throughout Masailand are expected to extend each other automatic hospitality, including sexual: visiting age mates may sleep with their host's wife. Conversely, the incest taboo is extended on an age-set basis: under penalty of severe beating, the burning of his homestead, and the slaughtering of his cattle, no person is allowed to marry or fornicate with a daughter of a member of his age set nor with any wife of a member of his father's age set. Age sets are named, and these age-set names are the principal historical milestones in Masai oral tradition.

When a new age set is opened at time X_1, the previous warrior age set goes through a series of rituals by which the warriors accede to junior elder status. They exchange their

---

many other societies, corporate age groupings play a key role in political, military, religious, and economic organization.

long-bladed warrior spears for short-bladed ones, they are allowed to own cattle, to marry, and to establish their own homestead, and they are freed from dietary taboos. The prior distinctions between the subsets of junior and senior warrior lose their significance, and for the rest of their lives, the set forms a unified whole. For the fifteen-year duration of the X_1 initiation cycle, the age set initiated during the X cycle belongs to the age grade of junior elders, a position they hold while roughly thirty to forty-five years of age. In the prime of their middle age, men are primarily concerned with marrying, procreating, raising boys who will be initiated in the X_2 cycle, and accumulating cattle (as the primary mark of wealth and status, and the means to become polygynous). Junior elders constitute an army reserve during raids, but they are relieved from the brunt of the fighting, which falls to the senior warriors. Junior eldership is thus a time devoted primarily to private domestic concerns, sandwiched between two long periods of civic duties, first as warriors, then as ruling class.

Fifteen years later, with the opening of the X_2 initiation cycle, every age set is again promoted into the next most senior age grade. The surviving junior elders now become the senior elders, with again a marked change in their status and functions. Senior elders, aged forty-five to sixty, are in their late middle age; they are experienced but not senile. They constitute the ruling age grade and their lives are devoted principally to public affairs, notably to running the entire initiation system with its multiple ritual and pedagogical tasks, and, hence, controlling the whole age-grade system, which forms the basis for Masai social organization. Naturally, age attrition in a society that has a high mortality rate through disease, war, and accidents (as occur in lion hunting, a test of manly courage) insures that senior elders are far fewer than warriors and junior elders; however, in keeping with the democratic conception of the Masai political order, power is decentralized, and leadership is shared and hemmed in by custom. There is no arbitrary use of power, and all adult men have some say in the collective decision making. Thus, the system cannot really be called oligarchic, because executive functions are not centralized enough to allow the use of a concept of state. Nor, interestingly enough, is it gerontocratic, for it is not the oldest men who are in positions of authority, but the ones in late middle age. True gerontocracy, as practiced, for example, in the College of Cardinals of the Roman Catholic Church, is a very exceptional political arrangement anywhere in the world. Power is typically vested in men in their late middle age, but far short of senility.

When, after another fifteen or sixteen years, the time comes for the opening of the X_3 initiating cycle, the surviving senior elders gracefully retire from active political life and become respected old men, consulted in matters of tradition, but otherwise without any direct ritual or political role. At any given time, there are typically a few surviving members of three superannuated age sets living in such esteemed retirement.

The central role of age stratification for Masai males, then, is in allocating social roles. In the simplest and most schematic terms, Masai males are stratified into five broad age categories: uninitiated children; initiated warriors (junior and senior); early middle-aged men concerned with procreation and domestic affairs; late middle-aged men devoted to public affairs; and old men in retirement. This age stratification system cuts completely across lineage membership, but it is integrated with the kinship system, since incest prohibitions and other constraints based on generation (for example, that fathers and sons may not belong to adjacent age sets) are extended to the age-grade system.

Perhaps most interestingly, this elaborate age-stratification system is probably the most democratic way of integrating large numbers of people (several hundred thousands) into a single, identifiable, self-conscious nation. Of course, as in all human societies, the democracy is limited by sex: for all intents and purposes, women are excluded from public life, except as wives and bearers of children. But the male Masai is indeed a free man. Neither tyrant nor slave, he earned the respect and admiration even of colonial administrators, and indeed became a colonial legend. It is ironic that now, as citizens of one of the more progressive African states (Tanzania), devoted to notions of freedom (*uhuru*) and egalitarian communalism (*ujamma*), the proud Masai are subjected to the assaults of a misguided neocolonial bureaucracy eager to "civilize" them and to make them till the soil. In 1968, a puritanical Area Commissioner, with the approval of President Julius Nyerere, even attempted to force Masai men to wear pants because he was afraid that camera-happy tourists might perpetuate stereotypes about Africa's being inhabited by naked savages. The same bureaucrat, incidentally, also banned on moral grounds emancipated urban women's wearing miniskirts in his district. The fate of the Masai at the hands of the neocolonial black bureaucracy is all the more ironic, since the Masai represent in purest form the ideal of African Socialism propounded by Nyerere, indeed in much purer form than the more "civilized" and "progressive" ethnic groups from which their new overlords come.

6 The Dynamics of Age and Sex Conflicts

In the last two chapters, we examined cross-culturally the parameters of age and sex differentiation. We explored the range of variability and the areas of overlap in the ways human societies have used and elaborated on the potentialities of biologically-based age and sex differences. In so doing, we have treated age and sex as two distinct phenomena, and we have dealt primarily with their structures. That is, we have discussed the question of how age and sex differences have been reflected in the structure of various societies.

Now, we shall turn to a more complex set of problems. First, we shall study the links between age and sex differentiation. Both are universal, and thus they always coexist, often in a relationship of close interdependence. Then, we shall relate both age and sex to other forms of social differentiation, such as kin group, caste, race, ethnicity, and class. Last, we shall examine the dynamics of age and sex differentiation—we shall explore age and sex as sources of social change. Marx was not the first social scientist to note that inequality led to conflict and conflict to change, but he was the first to expand these insights into the basis of his theoretical system. Since age and sex differentiation are always to some extent invidious, we can expect both age and sex to be sources of conflict and change, and indeed, they are.

Age and sex, the two universal ways of differentiating humans, are closely interrelated. There are numerous societies in which women, irrespective of their age, are treated as children in many essential respects. That is, women are held never to grow up, at least in terms of civic responsibility. The same device of perpetually relegating a whole subordinate social category to infantile status has been used also in other forms of stratification. For example, adult blacks in the southern United States were, until recently, called "boy" and "girl," and servants, serfs, or slaves are often treated as children. Preventing women from meaningful participation in public affairs, and confining their roles to the domestic sphere is an extremely common situation. As expressed in the traditional German motto, the place of women is held to be *Küche, Kinder und Kirche*. Even so far as the church is concerned, women are kept strictly in the passive and subordinate position of worshippers. The clergy is a male monopoly. In a great many societies, women and children share much the same political and legal disabilities: they may not vote, hold political office, wage war, be competent witnesses in court, administer or dispose of property, sign a binding contract, or engage in other acts that imply civic responsibility.

In short, women are almost universally domesticated—that is, their activities are largely confined to the familial sphere where they typically have authority over children, but where, in common with children, they are represented in public affairs by an adult male in authority: a husband or a father in a bilateral or patrilineal system, a brother or a mother's brother in matrilineal societies. Males are held to achieve full adult responsibility in public affairs after their initiation, marriage, fatherhood, or some such test of social maturity, whereas females typically are not.

At first blush, it is rather surprising that women have so consistently been identified with children when they so obviously share less with boys than they do with men. The term *patriarchy* often applied to the phenomenon and recently adopted as a feminist epithet is misleading, or at least ethnocentric, because it is often not the father (but rather the husband, husband's father, brother, or mother's brother) who has authority over the adult female; simply, it is an adult male who has authority over females and children. For lack of a better term, we may call this *viriarchy* (rule by men). Our surprise should increase when we note that the very same device of treating adults as infants has also been regularly used against adult *males* of politically subordinate groups in systems of class, caste, ethnic, or racial stratification. (In this case, the phenomenon has often been called *paternalism*.) Slaves, serfs, and subordinate ethnic or racial groups have often been disenfranchised, excluded from political office, disqualified as witnesses, jurors, heirs, or guardians, addressed in the same "familiar" form (*tu, Du*) as that used for children, and held to be immature, childish, emotional, irresponsible, unreliable, and so on. Many of the so-called democracies have been paternalistic, from ancient Athens to the contemporary United States. (These political systems in which representative government has been limited by race, ethnicity, or some such ascriptive criterion, I have elsewhere [1967] called "*Herrenvolk* democracies.")

Thus, it seems that the primordial inequality exists between adults and children, and that parental authority, for all its social legitimation by adults, is thus the fundamental model for human tyranny. That such a tyranny is rooted in physiology is equally clear: by the time an infant is two years old, and he is mature enough to have a means of expressing his will through speech and locomotion, he has understood that until he grows up, he stands no chance in a power contest with adults. Of course, adult power, as any human power, is not *purely* based on brute strength but results from a combination of physical strength and knowledge gained through experience and learning. Children, lacking both experience and strength, cannot effectively challenge adults. They are not only weak but they must "learn the ropes" in a system in which adults have a generation's headstart.

Shocking though it may seem to most parents, parental power is the most naked form of social coercion, tempered, to be sure, by love; but then, what is more arbitrary than love backed by power, and what is arbitrariness if not the condition of ultimate power? Love may exclude malevolence in the exercise of power and thus make tyranny tolerable, but it does not change the power disparity. Without love, tyranny becomes ghastly, as witnessed by orphanages and similar prisonlike institutions. Between adult males and females, the disparity in sheer brute strength is less than exists between adults and children, and the biological basis of power inequality is greatly elaborated by a cultural superstructure. Seen in that light, however, it is not surprising that the prototype of age inequality has been extended to sex: women share with children the fact that they have, on the whole, quite a few kilograms of muscle less than men, a disparity in strength that becomes all the greater when they must carry and protect an infant.

The argument that sex inequality takes second place to age inequality rather than vice versa is supported by the fact that the typical dominance order in human societies is adult males over adult females over children of both sexes. Females typically dominate those males whom they outweigh. The same situation prevails among nonhuman primates. Even in the Western folklore of the "war of the sexes," the exceptional woman who dominates her mate is almost invariably depicted as large and brandishing that female equivalent to the policeman's nightstick, the dough roller. Similarly, it is interesting that in Western societies, a far more powerful social stigma attaches to deviation from average height which reduces sexual dimorphism, than to a deviation that accentuates it. Tall women and short men are far more stigmatized than short women and tall men.

Perhaps the more parsimonious way of stating the relationship is that dominance correlates closely with physical strength, and that since strength disparities based on age are far greater than those based on sex, age differentiation is more pronounced. There is one flaw in this extreme physical-reductionist argument, however; namely, that *Homo sapiens* has used his intelligence to develop many forms of inequality not based on raw, unaided physical strength. The purest form of domination by virtue of brute strength (reinforced by disparities in knowledge and experience) prevails between adults and children. Strangely, adult domination has so far been almost unchallenged by organized social reform movements. It is constantly challenged by children at home, of course, but as children grow up, they are automatically "coopted" into adulthood, and before they grow up, they are not taken seriously. Thus, every generation of children has to fight all over again its hopelessly one-sided struggle against adult tyranny.

The subordination and domestication of women, on the other hand, goes much beyond its biological basis in sexual dimorphism. Women in any society, politically conscious and organized, could be a revolutionary force of far greater power than children could ever dream of becoming. Furthermore, the age-based model of domination has been extended to groups in which there are no biological differences in strength, and the subordinate group may greatly outnumber the dominant one, for example, between masters and slaves. At least provisionally, then, we may accept the hypothesis that the model of adult domination based predominantly on physical strength has been extended to sex, in which biological differences are far smaller, and to other forms of invidious status distinctions, in which biology plays no role at all.

The thesis of the interrelatedness of sex, age, and other forms of domination has received empirical confirmation in Stephens' work (1963). Stephens finds that husband-wife deference etiquette is more pronounced when father-son deference is also stressed. He observes also a close relationship between an autocratic state and an autocratic family structure. Autocratic agrarian states tend to be strongly male-adult dominated. Stephens suggests, however, that the autocracy of the state spreads to the family, rather than the basic model of familial tyranny's becoming elaborated into governmental forms.

This raises the question, then, of what, besides sexual dimorphism and the physical incapacitation of pregnancy and child care, keeps women subjugated. The answer is clear—marriage and the institution of the family, both human universals or near-universals. We have already seen that the specific form of marriage (polygyny, monogamy, polyandry) bears no simple relationship to the relative societal positions of men and women. But this is not to say that marriage and the family *in themselves* are not powerful contributory factors to the subordination of women. Indeed, they are. The family, whatever its form, establishes a basic dichotomy between the domestic sphere, in which women and children are largely confined, and a public sphere, which is the monopoly or near-monopoly of men. Because the public sphere consists of those legal, political, military, economic, religious, and other institutions that regulate the relations among kin groups, and between the entire society and the outside world, it always has preeminence over the domestic sphere. Even within the family, the authority of women is usually restricted to children, and the overall authority over the kin group is vested in men.

Marriage is almost invariably an unequal relationship between husband and wife. Stephens (1963), in a study of thirty-one societies, found that in twenty-one of them the husband was clearly dominant; in six societies he was mildly dominant; and only in five of them was there an approximately equal sharing of authority. Even in the latter cases, this equal sharing applied only to the domestic sphere. Males were everywhere dominant in the public sphere. In many societies, a woman has little, if any, choice of marriage partner, or even little say over whether she wants to marry at all. Marriage is an *obligation* in most societies, or, at least, the alternatives are powerfully stigmatized. Spinsterhood, illegitimacy, barrenness, and prostitution, the basic alternatives to marriage that most societies offer to women, frequently result in severe loss of status and ostracism. It might be argued quite accurately that, in many societies, the young man has no more freedom of choice of marital partner than does the young woman. Thus, quite a number of societies practice preferential cross-cousin marriage: it is strongly preferred that a young man marry his mother's brother's or his father's sister's daughter.[1] Even in these highly constraining systems of marriage, however, the initiative typically rests with men—if not with the groom, then with his male kinsmen. Women are basically exchanged between kin groups by men who, being prohibited by exogamy rules from marrying within the kin group, swap daughters and sisters against wives (Lévi-Strauss, 1968).

---

[1] One of the peculiarities of cross-cousin marriage in systems of unilineal descent (where they normally occur) is that, while enjoining or encouraging marriage between close relatives, such unions automatically enforce the rule of lineage and clan *exogamy*, since a cross-cousin can never belong to the same lineage or clan as oneself. Thus, paradoxical as it may seem at first glance, a rule of exogamy can be accompanied by preferential marriage to close relatives, and, conversely, as in the case of traditional North Indian Hinduism, strict rules of caste endogamy accompany extensive prohibitions against consanguineal marriages.

Another factor consolidating the subordination of women in marriage is that almost invariably wives are younger than husbands, and sometimes considerably so. Thus, lower status on the basis of sex is reinforced by lower status on the basis of age. This extremely widespread fact, partly based perhaps on the slightly earlier onset of puberty among females, points to the importance of studying age and sex differentiation in relation to each other. The physiological difference in the speed of sexual maturation is clearly not a sufficient explanation, for, in a few societies, marriage antedates the puberty of both partners, and, more commonly, females get married shortly after puberty, whereas for males, first marriage is often postponed for nearly a decade after puberty. Moreover, in polygynous societies (the majority), age disparity between husband and wife typically increases with each of the man's successive marriages. Marital age difference in favor of males increases both polygyny and the subordination of women. Again, this is not to say that there is a causal link between polygyny and the status of women; as we have seen, cross-cultural evidence reveals little, if any, such relationship.

Equally interesting is the link between a woman's age and her status. In a number of societies, women acquire higher status with age, including status over younger adult males. In some cases, women past the menopause can achieve even quasi-male privileges and status. In Western societies, for example, there is an extensive folklore of older women's dominating their husbands, sons, or sons-in-law.

There is an important reverse side to this linkage between age and sex status. To the extent that women are subordinated to men, their status is considerably determined by their value to men as reproductive and sexual agents. Since both of these properties are closely tied to age, it follows that the status of a female based on her nubility rises sharply at puberty, stays at a high plateau for ten to fifteen years, and then declines at a steadily accelerating rate. Growing old has far fewer saving graces for women than for men, and this is especially true in Western societies, where advanced age has few compensations, and where the position of a woman is so heavily dependent on her erotic relationship to the husband-breadwinner-head of the nuclear family.

Age and sex are not only linked to each other, but they are also linked to other forms of social differentiation, notably those based on ethnicity, race, caste, and class. There are two basic ways to state the problem. First, we can ask: How important are age and sex compared to other bases of differentiation? This is a rather uninteresting question, though, because it is practically tautological that there is an inverse correlation between the importance of age and sex differences and the general level of differentiation in a society.

That is, the more differentiated the society, the less important are age and sex relative to other differences. Clearly, in the most undifferentiated societies, such as Congo rain forest pygmies—where social relationships are defined almost entirely by marriage, kinship, age, and sex—the latter two are very important. Conversely, in complex agrarian societies, such as in India, where we find differentiation and stratification by religion, language, caste, and class, the importance of age and sex differences is relatively smaller.

A second, much less tautological, question is the following: Does the general level of social differentiation affect the magnitude of age and sex differences? Instead of asking how important it is in Society A to be a *man*, compared to being a Brahmin, a black, or a doctor, we now ask whether the general complexity of Society A affects the relative differentiation of men versus women. As a gross generalization subject to a number of exceptions, we might say that differences in status between men and women tend to be greatest in the upper middle of the differentiation continuum, that is, in preindustrial, class-stratified, agrarian societies. Both the simpler hunting and pastoralist societies and the more complex industrial ones seem to be more sex egalitarian. Among Congo pygmies, for instance, Turnbull (1961, 1965) reports nearly egalitarian relations between men and women, and a rather blurred sexual division of labor; both men and women engage in hunting and collecting, the men doing most but not all of the former, and the women doing most but not all of the latter.

Age differentiation seems sharpest in the nomadic, pastoralist, bellicose societies, such as the East African age-set societies we have discussed. On the differentiation continuum, age seems to "peak" in both absolute and relative magnitude one or two steps before the crest in sex differentiation. This is probably due to the chronic state of war in many pastoralist societies. In the absence of a complex technology of destruction, the organization of young adult males into a permanent war machine becomes a crucial competitive advantage. This generates roles and statuses sharply differentiated by age, since fighting ability declines steeply with age when military technology is simple.

Marriage is probably the best institution in which to study the interplay between age, sex, and other forms of differentiation. Matrimony is always circumscribed by a set of rules determining whom one must, may, or may not marry. These rules typically involve most of the important bases of social differentiation.[2] The specific rules vary enormously from

---

[2] A lexicographic footnote is in order here. A marriage rule is said to be *prescriptive* if its violation calls for

society to society, but in all societies, marriage is far too important a matter to be left to the whim of the prospective spouses. Some marriage systems are extremely restrictive, leaving very little choice of acceptable spouses, for example, in traditional Hinduism or in societies that have preferential cross-cousin marriage; others are much less constraining, for example, Western industrial societies. In all societies, however, some categories of relatives are subject to an incest taboo; in addition, there are a number of norms defining certain matches as more desirable than others, or indeed prescribing or proscribing them altogether.

Generally, corporate kin groups in systems of unilineal descent (that is, lineages and clans, whether patri- or matrilineal) are *exogamous*, although there are a number of exceptions. These groups are sometimes hierarchized, but more often they are not. Ethnic, racial, caste, and class groups, on the other hand, which are typically hierarchized, tend to be *endogamous* (either preferentially or prescriptively). The most common deviation from the endogamous tendency of hierarchized groups, however is hypergamy. There are far more cases when it is acceptable for a woman to marry "up" rather than to marry "down."

The widespread prevalence of hypergamy over hypogamy bears directly on the interrelation between sex and class status. In hypergamy, the superior class status of the husband reinforces his sex status, whereas, in the case of hypogamy, there results what sociologists have called *status inconsistency*, that is, a situation in which various status differences function in opposite directions. Frequently combined with preferential polygyny, hypergamy creates a close relationship between the number of wives a man has and his social status (as well as his age). In most polygynous and stratified societies, men from the upper strata may marry women from the lower strata as well as from their own status group, whereas

---

severe penalties and *preferential* if the sanctions are mild. *Endogamy* is a rule that determines the social group within which one must or should marry; *exogamy* defines the group out of which one should or must marry. All societies have rules of both exogamy and endogamy, applied, of course, to different types of groups. Descent groups such as lineages and clans are generally (but not always) exogamous, whereas ethnic, racial, and class groups tend to be at least preferentially and sometimes prescriptively endogamous. For hierarchized groups, when the woman marries a husband of higher status than herself, *hypergamy* is said to result; marriage between partners of equal status is called *isogamy*; and when the wife is of higher status than the husband, the union is called *hypogamous*.

97 Dynamics of Age and Sex Conflicts

upper status women are usually confined to marrying their social equals. Even in the much rarer cases of hypogamy, the higher status wife typically does not dominate her husband, but rather loses status. As a rule, the husband determines the class status of the couple, so that even in cases of hypogamy, male dominance frequently takes precedence over class differences.

Thus, in the typical polygynous, stratified society, men may choose as wives women from all strata equal to or lower than their own. Because marriage is often accompanied by the payment of bridewealth, and wealth and social status are also a function of age, there is frequently a close relationship between polygyny on the one hand, and age *and* social status on the other. Polygyny is characteristically a privilege of older, higher status men.

A high class status confers not only marital privileges on men, but also rights of sexual access to lower status women. There too, male dominance is reinforced by class differences. Concubinage between high status men and low status women is a phenomenon quite distinct from polygyny; indeed, it is often found in monogamous societies. Nearly all of the so-called miscegenation that took place in the slave regimes of the Western Hemisphere, for example, was the product of concubinage between white masters or overseers and female slaves. Similarly, female domestic servants were often in a difficult position to deny sexual access to their employers. European nineteenth-century novels are filled with maids who get pregnant by the son of the household and are married off to the coachman, and with students of breeding who have affairs with seamstresses who, with some luck, later marry a solid journeyman, or if unlucky, end up as streetwalkers. To mention another example from Western history, the *jus primae noctis* (right to the first night) or *droit de cuissage* (right to the thigh), whereby a feudal lord had the right to deflower his villein (peasant) maidens on their wedding night, was well established in parts of Medieval and Renaissance Europe.

Two points relating to the position of women are worth noting. First, polygyny frequently insures a more secure and dignified position to women than the concubinage *cum* monogamy system just described. The low status wife of a polygynous husband has, by definition, all kinds of legal rights which a low status concubine of some high status woman's monogamous husband does not have. Second, the marital and sexual privileges conferred by high class status are typically not extended to the females born into the high status group. Frequently, the reverse is true: the upper-class woman is far less free, at least sexually, than her lower-class sister, and she has far more limited options for a "suitable" marriage. In monogamous societies especially, the upper-class woman often must compete for the men of her social class with the sexually more attractive women from lower classes, and thus has a far higher probability of spinsterhood.

Upper-class women are usually more sheltered, kept in seclusion and denied freedom of movement, of association, and of sexual expression both before and after marriage, than lower status women. The latter, who are frequently forced to engage in productive activities, cannot afford the luxury of genteel, indolent seclusion, which is the lot of the women in the leisure class. It follows that the status disparity between men and women in the upper class is frequently much greater than among the peasantry and working classes. Notwithstanding stereotypes, and an etiquette of "gallantry" to the contrary, upper class status for a woman is often a gilded cage in which she may share the material comfort and the leisure of the males of her class, but few of the freedoms enjoyed either by lower-class women or by her male class equals.

Thus, within a stratified society, the relative position of men and women may vary considerably from group to group, usually in favor of the low status group. For example, in the United States, the black female head of a "matrifocal" family (centered around the mother) may be in a better position *relative to the males of her group* than is a white middle-class suburban housewife. Of course, this does not imply that her total social position is enviable, because she suffers under the double disability of race and sex. This complex interplay among sex, age, and other dimensions of status highlights the difficulty of making cross-cultural comparisons, unless one clearly specifies what one compares to what and on which dimensions.

Last, we shall examine the role of age and sex differentiation in the genesis of conflict and change. One of the few generalizations that holds almost universally in social science is that people resent being in an inferior position. Only under certain conditions, however, does perceived inferiority and its consequent resentment result in group consciousness and conflict. That status distinctions based on age and sex are universally perceived is well established. That they frequently lead to strains and conflict is also evident and has long given rise to theorizing by social scientists from Freud to Radcliffe-Brown. Freud, for example, attributed the "Oedipal" relationship between father and son to sexual rivalry over the mother-wife, and propounded a male-biased theory of sexual conflict based on the alleged superiority of the penis over the female genitalia and the envy that the lack of a penis is supposed to unleash in females. Radcliffe-Brown (1952) and others after him (Homans & Schneider, 1955) have argued against Freud's sexual interpretation of father-son conflicts. They noted that in matrilineal societies in which authority over the male ego is vested in his mother's brother and not in his father, the same kind of ambivalent relationship prevails between ego and his mother's brother as between father and son in patrilineal or bilateral societies; conversely, the father-son relationship tends to be warm and affectionate. In patrilineal societies, on the other hand, the "Oedipal" syndrome of ambivalence is manifested between father and son, while the mother's brother plays the warm affective role of "male mother." Radcliffe-Brown concluded, reasonably enough, that these feelings were determined not by hypothetical incestuous and parricidal desires on the part of monstrous little boys, but by sheer resentment of whoever wields the symbolic or actual stick over little boys' heads. In simple terms, power inhibits love and promotes strain.

Sex and generational conflicts are evident and ubiquitous enough, both in societies at large, and in their constituent families. The family, romanticized and idealized *ad nauseam* by sociologists as the cornerstone of society and the bedrock of social stability, could just as convincingly be presented as a petty tyranny made up of bickering spouses and cowering children held together, if at all, by the arbitrary power of its adult male head.[3] Both marital and intergenerational harmony seem to be the exception rather than the rule, as shown, for instance, by the high incidence of divorce in societies where sanctions against divorce are relatively mild.

Yet, equally evident is the fact that conflicts based on age and sex characteristically lead to rebellion as distinguished from revolution. (By rebellion, I mean a movement that aims at changing the persons in power, whereas a revolution seeks to change the system.) In the next chapter, we shall examine the extent to which the youth and the feminist movements in contemporary industrial societies may be revolutionary. Generally, however, sex and generational conflicts do not in any fundamental way threaten the existing order. Though ubiquitous, they are typically channeled in well-defined, predictable, indeed ritualized, ways. The ritualization of conflict has concerned social scientists for years (Gluckman, 1954; Norbeck, 1963; van den Berghe, 1963), because it constitutes an effective way of handling chronic sources of tension without posing any threat to the existing order.

---

[3] In the Marxist tradition represented especially by Engels (1942) and Bebel (1923), the origins of the family and patriarchy are associated with the development of private property, and the bourgeois family's institution of property inheritance is presented as the ultimate locus of inequality. But the mainstream of sociology and anthropology has certainly taken a very benign view of the family in general, and the monogamous family in particular, as the basic building block of society and the cornerstone of the social order.

In most societies, certain forms of behavior that would otherwise be regarded as reprehensible become permissible or even expected under particular well-defined conditions. Many of these "rituals of rebellion" reverse the roles, especially age and sex roles, between unequal status groups. In some African societies, for example, women, on certain ritual occasions, are expected to dress and behave like men. Among the Gahuku of New Guinea, a patrilineal society in which the status of women is relatively low, women engage men in mock battle during marriage negotiations. When the kinsmen of the bride return from the groom's village laden with the bridewealth pigs, their own women ambush them on the way, bombard them with projectiles, and attempt to bludgeon to death the pigs which are later communally eaten by the men and women of the bride's village (Read, 1965). Or, to mention an example from Western society, occasionally at dances, a time may be set aside for "ladies' choice," when the usual pattern of men's inviting women to dance is reversed.

Similarly, generational conflicts also find a channelled expression in such role reversals. The "trick or treat" rituals of Halloween are a case in point in American society. In boarding schools, where conditions of rigid regimentation exacerbate conflicts between age groups, there are often ceremonial occasions, such as an end-of-year theatrical performance, during which pupils may lampoon their teachers with impunity. The simplest explanation for this kind of ritualized status reversal is that it operates as a safety valve. It gives vent in a perfectly harmless way to the accumulated resentment caused by status inequalities, and thus serves to manage conflict and in the process, to prevent change. Indeed, ritualized rebellion, by stressing the exceptional character and the permissible limits of the status reversal, serves to reinforce by contrast the hierarchy that prevails most of the time (van den Berghe, 1963).

Paradoxically, the existence of such rituals of rebellion in a given situation is a very good indication that the status order is firmly entrenched. The ostensible reversal of the "normal" order under circumscribed conditions is a reaffirmation in a negative form of what the proper status order is. To illustrate from personal experience, in the department of sociology of which I am a member, there existed an annual ritual known as the "Monster Rally," organized jointly by incoming faculty members and graduate students. The event was in part an initiation ritual for incoming members, but it also included graduate students' skits lampooning faculty. This ritual became defunct, however, in the late 1960s, when the students' challenge to faculty authority became widespread and organized enough to make the students look at the Monster Rally no longer as a satisfying yet safe way of expressing criticism of their elders, but as a silly waste of time when there was real power to be gained through political action. A series of constitutional meetings between faculty and graduate students took place, in which mechanisms of student cooptation and consultation reminiscent of colonial regimes in Africa were evolved. In the end, the students gained very little power, but it took them some time to realize it, and at the time, they saw themselves as fundamentally challenging the status quo. Curiously, one form of institutionalized conflict between faculty and graduate students survived the political crisis, namely the faculty-student baseball game. Perhaps sport is the opium of revolutionaries, to paraphrase Raymond Aron.

Besides rituals of rebellion, age and sex conflicts are expressed also through other forms of channelled aggression. In a number of rigidly age-graded societies, for example, institutionalized rivalry among age sets is an important feature of the system. We have seen how mock battles resulting in wounds were an expected form of rivalry between junior and senior warriors among the Masai. The hazing of "plebes" by upper classmen at the United States Military Academy, or its equivalent in countless fraternities, boarding schools, and other such age-graded establishments are all highly patterned ways of expressing conflict between hierarchized age groups. Sport competition is a peculiarly recurrent device in this respect; indeed, what is competitive team sport but mock combat, that is, a form of conflict in which the damage inflicted, both moral and physical, is carefully circumscribed?

Yet another form of expressing conflict is humor. The repertory of sexual jokes is extremely wide in Western cultures, and in many other cultures as well. Sexual jokes, it should be noted, frequently have both a sex-erotic and a sex-gender content—the joke revolves around not only the sexual activity as such, but also around the gender-linked roles of the characters. In the Western folklore, most sexual or "dirty" jokes are, in fact, antifeminist, treating women as sex objects or ridiculing women's alleged foibles, sexual desires, or attempts to emulate or seek equality with men. From its inception as an organized political movement in the nineteenth century, feminism has been the butt of ridicule. Sex segregation is another interesting feature of Western sexual jokes and bantering. "Off-color" jokes are deemed fit to be told only in male company, ostensibly to protect the purity and delicate sensibilities of women, but, in fact, because most of these jokes are degrading and hence offensive to women. The similarity of sexual jokes with ethnic and racial jokes in this respect is striking, and it is certainly no coincidence that there is a considerable degree of overlap between these two categories of humor. As for mother-in-law jokes, they may owe their popularity partly to the fact that they revolve around both sex and generational conflicts.

Why do age and sex conflicts so seldom lead to revolutionary change? Why do age and sex so seldom form the basis of mass solidarity and lead to political polarization? As far as sex is concerned, the main factor is probably the set of binary ties linking individual males and females to each other in a particularly intimate, all-encompassing, and long-lasting relationship. This basic fact was recognized a century ago by John Stuart Mill (1869). So long as the vast majority of adult women in any given society allow themselves to be linked in a marital or amorous relationship with adult males, it will be difficult for them to join other women in fighting men. Heterosexual love, and indeed, probably all love, is fundamentally counterrevolutionary. The greatest revolutionary lovers of humanity in the abstract have often been confirmed misanthropists, and, given half a chance, frightful tyrants.

Regarding age or generational conflicts, the answer probably lies first in the high degree of physical and emotional dependency of children on adults, and second in the lack of political competence and experience of children. These factors, of course, would not preclude polarized age conflicts between younger and older adults, and indeed, strife among adult generations is common enough. But, surprisingly, this strife typically takes the form of the younger adults' accelerating the retirement of the older ones, thereby leading to a periodic rejuvenation of personnel but not to an alteration in the system. Again, this conflict is more akin to rebellion than to revolution. The nonrevolutionary character of age conflicts may, in the last analysis, be due to the trite but inescapable fact that the young grow old if they only live long enough. One may push for earlier entry into the ruling age class, but why should one overthrow a system that guarantees one a privileged place in it simply if one stays alive? This is all the truer when the cost of opposing the system may well be that one does not survive to enjoy what one otherwise would obtain at no risk. The proletarian has nothing to lose but his chains; the young man has but his impatience to lose. Unlike other underprivileged groups, all the young have to do to be promoted out of their lowly station is to "wait until they grow up," a prospect that all astute parents know how to dangle in front of their progeny's noses with a predictably pacifying effect.

Being female has, of course, a quality of permanence that could fan the coals of revolution, but until such time as militant feminists will propose a means (satisfying to most women) of dispensing with men, the majority of sisters can be predicted to sell out to the enemy. Until such time, the strategy of female liberation will have to be one of reeducation of, and cooperation between, both sexes, as distinguished from the revolutionary model of class struggle.

Dynamics of Age and Sex Conflicts

So far, we have paid no special attention to industrial societies, on the assumption that the whole spectrum of human experience is of considerable import to us in the industrial West. All the same, industrial societies are both exceptional and, through their destructive, polluting, and predatory capabilities, consequential not only to their own members, but to everyone else as well. At any rate, they are worth a chapter to themselves.

7 Industrial Societies

Often, industrial technology is argued to be man's (and woman's) Great Emancipator. Technology, so the argument goes, emancipates man from the drudgery of physical labor, and automation may free him from any labor at all, leaving him ever-increasing time for leisure. Industry made serfdom, slavery, and child labor obsolete, led to a general increase in standards of living, and to an appreciable narrowing of disparities in income distribution among social classes. By reducing the significance of brute strength and increasing the importance of skill and education, advanced technology has resulted in lengthened and more equally accessible education and all but eliminated the advantage of males over females in productivity. Translated into the lyricism of consumerism and the affluent society, this paean to technology conjures the vision of a streamlined, automated, sanitized, push-button world in which man, woman, and child, freed of work, want, and disease, will be able to devote most of their time to the pursuit of pleasure, and perhaps to the cultivation of their creative talents. The female version of the consumerist vision, so diligently advanced by the advertising industry, pictures the suburban housewife effortlessly breezing through her aseptic and luxurious dwelling, cheerfully controlling her army of mechanical slaves (simple enough to operate so as to spare her mental as well as physical effort), and occupying much of her abundant leisure grooming herself into an acceptable facsimile of the deodorized, seductive simpleton whom her harried, junior-executive mate expects to find when he comes home from a hard day at the office.

Television commercials are not an accurate representation of American society, of course. But it is evident that, myths of matriarchy to the contrary, American women are generally less emancipated than those of a number of less technologically developed societies. Relative to men in their own society, American women have made no substantial gains in status since the Nineteenth Amendment of 1920 legalizing women's suffrage. Even that modest accomplishment, rendered nearly meaningless in a political system that gives the voters little real choice, took over half a century of campaigning to achieve.

This is not to say that sex roles have not changed in the recent history of industrial societies. In some countries, for example, in Scandinavia, Israel, Japan, and most of the socialist countries, women have made significant gains during the last half-century, but, in most of the Western capitalist countries, the legal victories of the nineteenth and early twentieth centuries have not been followed by an appreciable improvement in women's status. Holter (1971) concludes that sex equality requires both socialism and a high level of technology. She summarizes also what she sees as five major changes in sex roles in the transition from "traditional" to "industrial" societies. First, whereas previously sex roles were overtly unequal, there now exist an ideology of equality and a formal legal equality that render sex discrimination more covert. Second, there was a shift from an unreflecting acceptance of sex inequality as the natural state of things to a self-awareness or sex-consciousness questioning the legitimacy of sex inequality. Third, the burden of maintaining sex inequality has shifted from an ideology of sex inequality to differences in the socialization of boys and girls. Fourth, there has been a shift from supernatural to rational premises in accounting for differences in sex roles. Finally, the repertory of sex roles for both men and women within a single society has become more varied.

In short, Holter suggests both an ideological shift toward egalitarianism and a greater range of sex roles for both sexes as a result of general social differentiation. Like any dichotomous distinction between "traditional" and "industrial" or "modern" societies, Holter's does not take into account the enormous cultural diversity within each category, and her characterizations are limited probably to Western societies during the last two centuries.

The term *feminism*, coined in 1872 by Alexandre Dumas the younger in his pamphlet, *L'Homme-Femme*, is only a century old. Conscious, organized protests by groups of women rebelling against social conditions is much older, and undoubtedly occurred in a great many non-Western societies. In Western history, we have a 2400-year record of sexual politics, and it is ironic that much of what has survived of this struggle has consisted of comedies by male satirists from Aristophanes to Molière. Not until George Bernard Shaw has the joke been on the men.

For all the historical antecedants, a uniquely and sweepingly revolutionary way of thinking was germinating in the eighteenth-century salons of Paris. It gave rise to what is usually known as the Enlightenment, which spread with great speed to the rest of Western Europe and to the American colonies, and culminated politically in the French, American, and other bourgeois revolutions. Based on radical rationalism, skepticism, egalitarianism, and universalism, the Enlightenment was probably the greatest mental leap that humanity ever took to liberate itself from the intellectual shackles of ethnocentrism, intolerance, superstition, social privilege, and religious and political tyranny.

Naturally, this sweeping mental spring cleaning attacked the sexual dimension of privilege also, finding its political expression in the *Déclaration des Droits de l'Homme et du Citoyen* passed in 1789 by the French Constituent Assembly. Although French syntax was not purged of the male bias that makes it use the male gender to refer to both sexes of the species, by this time, there was considerable agreement among the leading minds of Europe and America that women should be treated on a footing of equality with men. The key role of women in the French Enlightenment is worth stressing. A witty, educated, intelligent woman stood at the center of every Parisian literary and intellectual salon, and although she undoubtedly did pass around many a teacup, she was also in most cases a respected participant in the discussions.

If we trace back the modern phase of feminism in Western societies to the eighteenth century, then the important fact emerges that the liberation of women has from the start been inextricably linked with the more universal cause of the liberation of mankind. For example, it is not merely coincidental that the Seneca Falls Convention of American Women took place during the "hot summer" of 1848, when the whole of Europe was in revolutionary turmoil. Nor is the close link between the mid-nineteenth-century American feminists and the Abolitionist movement fortuitous. To be sure, many prominent Abolitionists were male chauvinists (and, indeed, racists as well), but women activists played an important role in both the British and the American Abolitionist movement, and it was in part male chauvinism in the Abolitionist movement that spurred female militancy on the sexual front. The emancipation of women has been a salient feature also of the Socialist movement, and prominent women from Louise Michel to Rosa Luxemburg have been closely associated with it. The First World War and its immediate aftermath saw: the Bolshevik and Mexican Revolutions; Irish independence; abortive Socialist uprisings in Germany; in addition to the successful conclusion of the bourgeois Womens' Suffrage movement in the world's two leading capitalist countries (United Kingdom in 1917, United States in 1920). Finally, the resurgence of feminism in the United States during the last few years has not been unrelated to the civil rights movement and the youth movement.

Freedom is contagious; so, unfortunately, is nonsense. Thus, certain militant feminist groups in the United States have emulated the separatist logic of some black militants and developed a counter-sexist ideology akin to black racism. Just as some people have suggested that Black Studies are a separate field to be taught by blacks to blacks and for blacks to develop group identity, the same reasoning is currently being applied to Women's Studies. Furthermore, the tendency toward racial and ethnic separatism has split the feminist movement which, in the United States, is predominantly campus based and white middle class in composition. The relationship between women's liberation and other radical causes in the United States is thus paradoxical: while the consciousness of being oppressed spreads from one group to another, the ethnocentrism and parochialism so evident in the racial and ethnic movements divide the oppressed groups in their competition for scarce resources and prevent the growth of a universal ideology of liberation.

What changes have taken place in the status of women in industrial societies after more than a century of sexual politics? First, there seems to be no simple correlation between emancipation of women and degree of industrialization. If we define emancipation as the absence of sex-based disabilities or differences, either *de facto* or *de jure*, we find that the status of women is relatively low in some highly industrialized countries like Germany or Japan, and relatively high in less industrialized countries like the People's Republic of China or Albania. Industrially backward Albania, for example, elected 91 women out of 264 representatives in the People's Assembly (a little over one-third), a proportion far higher than in industrially advanced Japan, Germany, Britain, or the United States. Clearly, the ideological color of the regime is a more powerful determinant than level of industrialization or technology. Emancipation of women is one of the towering achievements of socialist countries, especially if one considers the prerevolutionary position of women in those societies.

Such global comparisons are difficult to make because there are many dimensions to sexual status (legal rights, economic status, political participation, decision making in the family, sexual morality), but it seems that the frequent association of female emancipation with industrialization is the result not of an empirical correlation but of our confusing two independent factors. The factor that concerns us is the position of women relative to men. It bears no relationship to the level of material comfort, health, well-being, and so on that women (and men) may enjoy in a given society. The Manhattan call girl in her air-conditioned luxury flat might never wish to trade jobs with her Soviet sister shovelling snow in -30 degree weather in Novosibirsk, despite the fact that her status relative to the men of her society is far inferior to that of the Soviet woman.

Industrial technology reduces the economic significance of sexual dimorphism and thus facilitates the creation of a social order in which a far greater equality of treatment and opportunity between men and women *could* be implemented. Most industrial societies have moved very slowly in that direction, even though they have greatly increased the standard of living of both sexes. Like the harem concubine, the suburban housewife may live in luxury, but that does not make her free; the black ghetto mother may live in squalor and misery but be relatively freer in relation to men.

No doubt a major change did take place during the last century of Western history, extending into other countries that have fallen under Western influence. The legal status of women has changed for the better as a consequence of the general ideological shift toward egalitarianism. This is especially evident in civic, parental, marital, and property rights. Although these changes are appreciable, the actual position of women in the distribution of power outside the domestic sphere and in the occupational world has remained remarkable stable. For example, even when the principle of "equal pay for equal work" is applied, sex discrimination in employment is preserved through wholesale occupational segregation: men and women are paid the same wages for the same job, but they hardly ever do the same job, and lowly-paid occupations are almost invariably defined as women's jobs.

Gross (1968) has extensively documented the stability of sex segregation in occupations in the United States. Compiling an index of sex segregation for over 300 occupations, he found virtually no change from 1900 to 1960. Around two-thirds of all female employees in each decade would have had to change jobs to exhibit the same sex distribution as men in those occupations. Although the proportion of women in the labor force increased vastly, the amount of occupational sex segregation remained constant. The increased proportion of women in the labor force was achieved through a combination of the rapid expansion of already existing female occupations, the creation of new occupations that were female from the start, and the displacement of males by females in some generally lowly-paid jobs. The range of jobs open to both men and women has become wider over time, but overall segregation has remained substantially unchanged.

The tendency toward sex segregation was somewhat modified, however, by discernible trends in opposite directions for male and female occupations: male jobs became more resistant to female entry over time, while female occupations became more open to male entry (Gross, 1968). It is interesting to note also that sex segregation in jobs is far greater than race segregation, although there are basic similarities in the ways in which both forms of prejudice operate and result in wage disparities. In 1960, for example, 46.8 percent of the nonwhites in the Gross sample of occupations would have had to change jobs to bring about a random racial distribution, whereas 68.4 percent of the women would have had to shift to effect random sex distribution.

Gross (1971) explored also the cross-cultural relationship between the rigidity of the sexual division of labor and the level of industrialization. Countries in which there was virtually no industrialization were excluded because of statistical unreliability of the data and the almost complete absence of women from the wage economy. The overall tendency, however, was for an *increasing* degree of sex segregation in wage occupations through the earlier and middle phases of industrialization, until a high plateau was reached. In the United States, this occurred around 1900. In any case, there is no evidence that industrialization results in the breakdown of occupational sex segregation.

When women "invade" male preserves, they are typically subjected to countless forms of discrimination, some subtle, others less so, but all very difficult to prove in court. The net result of *de facto* occupational segregation and extralegal and elusive discrimination is to impose a staggering economic penalty on women. In the United States, for example, the penalty paid in wages for being female is much greater than that for being black. The median earnings of all female civilian workers over fourteen years of age in 1968, for example, was only 38.9 percent of the median earnings of all male employees. This figure includes part-time workers, and many more women than men work part time. Full-time female workers earned 58.2 percent of full-time males' salaries. The very fact that more women work part time is, at least in part, a result of sex discrimination. By contrast, male black workers made 61.1 percent of what their white counterparts earned, female blacks earned 70.0 percent of female whites' salaries, and the racial difference was even smaller for full-time workers. (Blacks are overrepresented also in part-time jobs because of discrimination, but not nearly as much as are women.)

The main reason that so many women in industrial societies accept this blatant sex-based economic exploitation and discrimination is that they accept also the argument that it is the role of the adult male to be the breadwinner for the nuclear family. Female tolerance of domestication in the nuclear family and exploitation in the larger society are connected with a conception of marriage as an arrangement wherein the husband provides economic security for his "dependents." Many women look upon their jobs either as a premarital pastime or, later, as a marital supplement. In theory, alimony is supposed to cover the contingency of divorce. However, the real economic crunch for women comes for husbandless mothers who must support not only themselves but also their children. Along with the blacks and the old, single mothers constitute one of the larger underclasses of America, and of other industrial societies. In 1969, families with a female head earned a median income of only 48.2 percent of that of husband-wife families in the United States.

In the United States, a greatly disproportionate number of black women are heads of households with dependent children. In the 1970 census, some 19 percent of black women were separated or divorced compared to only 6 percent of white women. Thus, there is an overlap between sex and race discrimination: racial differentials are considerably reduced when the effect of sexual discrimination is taken out. Of the two forms of economic discrimination in the United States today, sexual discrimination has become not only the most widespread but also the most blatant and the most economically costly.

In sheer economic terms, then, women in industrial societies are the most exploited group, a massive and permanent proletariat in the literal as well as in the conventional sense. Far from alleviating that condition, industrialization, at least under capitalism, seems to have worsened it. This fact is obscured by the spectacular rise in living standards of the general population, a rise in which women have shared both directly and indirectly through kinship or marital association with breadwinning males. But, relative to males the status of women has, for the most part, not been favorably affected by industrial capitalism. This is hardly surprising if one considers that unpaid domestic service and child-rearing are by far the largest occupations of women even in the most industrialized societies. In a system of production in which the wage sector has become nearly all-encompassing for men, and in which the cost of services has skyrocketed, half or more of the adult women are still left out of the wage economy altogether, and those remaining are nearly all relegated to part-time and low paying jobs.

It is true that the married woman generally shares the income and standard of living of her breadwinning husband, and that the woman's structural position is very different from that of other large industrial underclasses, such as the urban proletariat or racial outcasts. It is equally true, however, that in societies that value work in direct relation to its monetary returns, women's domestic labor is lowly esteemed, at least by the standards of the larger society. The mother-wife may be "appreciated" in her home, but for extrafamilial purposes, her work does not count. Furthermore, there is little room in domestic work for social class differentiation: cleaning a $10,000 house is much the same as cleaning a $50,000 house. The latter may be better equipped, but then it is probably also larger. In either case, housework expands to fill the time available for its completion, as most "housewives" well know. The category of *housewife*, into which nearly all adult women are statistically lumped if they cannot demonstrate cash earnings, is illustrative of the industrial woman's economic role—she is a provider of unpaid sexual and housekeeping services for which she receives bed and board, being treated, of course, "as a member of the family." As an economic class, women are both atomized and kept on the fringes of wage employment by the nuclear family system. Although women are an easily identifiable class, the family system makes it difficult for them to become class-conscious and to organize in defense of their class interests.

Again, we return to the family, and more especially to the nuclear family, as the ultimate and intractable basis of female subordination. Far from emancipating women, industrialization has imprisoned them in nuclear families in which they have been increasingly cut off from associations with other adults of both sexes, and the absence of other adult women has destroyed the considerable degree of collective child-care that an extended and polygynous family offers. Of course, the schools have partially taken over child-raising functions, but not during infancy, and with birth spacing, a woman can have infant children for much of her young adulthood. In Rossi's words (1969):

> Behind the veneer of modern emancipation is a woman isolated in an apartment or suburban home, exclusively responsible for the care of young children, dependent on her husband for income, misled to believe that sex gratification is only possible via a vaginal orgasm simultaneous with male ejaculation, and urged to buy more and more clothes and household possessions, which she then takes more time but little pleasure in maintaining.

It is little wonder then, as Rossi (1969) and others have noted, that militant feminists have frequently come from the ranks of "unattached" women: the single, the divorced, or at least the childless. This phenomenon, facilely dismissed by male chauvinists as proof that only frustrated, unfeminine "bitches" in need of a good "lay" turn to feminism, has in fact far deeper structural roots.[1] In effect, the "attached" woman enters a compact with her husband in which she exchanges sexual favors and domestic labor for economic security. This arrangement is at the basis of the feminist thesis that there is not much difference between marriage and prostitution, or if there

---

[1] It is interesting to note how professional sociologists who otherwise show little inclination to seek psychologycal explanations of phenomena regress to the crudest kinds of Freudian psychologism when their prejudices are involved.

is a difference, it is in favor of the prostitute, who at least does not have to wash her client's clothes or shine his shoes.

In contrast, the "unattached" woman must fend economically for herself and her children; and, naturally, she is far more likely to become "sex-conscious" when she faces blatant discrimination in employment. Feminist activism in industrial societies thus shares many elements in common with the development of class consciousness. As Rossi (1969) puts it:

> The size of a women's rights movement has, therefore, been responsive to the proportion of "unattached" women in a population. An excess of females over males, a late age at marriage, postponement of childbearing, a high divorce rate, a low remarriage rate, and greater longevity for women, all increase the number of unattached women in a society, and therefore, increase the potential for sex equality activism.

The abolition of the bourgeois family to remedy sex and class inequality is an old socialist theme going back to Marx and Engels. After a brief and catastrophic attempt to implement this vision in the early, idealistic phase of the Bolshevik Revolution, the Stalinist counterrevolution reestablished all the major functions of the bourgeois family except the inheritance of property. Mitchell (1969) has presented perhaps the most creative feminist critique of the classical socialist position on female emancipation, with its heavy emphasis on the system of production as the cause of inequality. Her thesis is that the subjugation of women is based on a nexus of four types of social relations. The system of production is male-dominated and has remained stably so for the last few decades in industrial countries. The sexual, reproductive, and socializing functions, on the other hand, are defined as the woman's sphere and are combined in the family. Since these functions have biological underpinnings, women are socially defined as *natural* beings, in contradistinction to men, who dominate the eminently *social* system of production.

Mitchell concludes that the emancipation of women cannot be achieved simply through a more equal entry into the system of production, as the early socialists also recognized, but she goes beyond the old abstract slogan for the abolition of the bourgeois family. The liberation of women, she states, will result from the dissociation of sex, reproduction, and child socialization in the advanced industrial countries, which are the only ones meeting the necessary conditions for such a dissociation of hitherto familial functions. The techniques of contraception dissociate sex from reproduction; the techniques of artificial insemination, fetal implantation, and extrauterine reproduction will make it possible to dissociate reproduction from sexuality; finally, the trend toward greater extrafamilial socialization could ultimately dissociate the woman from child training. The focus of the attack should not, therefore, be on the family as such, but on the family as the institutional nexus of the biological underpinnings of human societies.

Mitchell's views lead to a fresh evolutionary perspective on the subject of sex differentiation. Thus, the much heralded "loss of function" of the "modern" family is largely a process whereby, in industrial societies, social institutions have become increasingly dichotomized into a macrosocial sphere with a complex network of interrelated, male-dominated, economic and political agencies, and a microsocial family sphere which is socially defined as "the woman's place." Since the residual functions of the family have the most clearly biological bases, this social evolution has, in fact, resulted in a sharper nature-culture and male-female polarity than in less differentiated preindustrial societies. Women have been left holding the laundry basket while men hold the bread basket. To a great extent, socialist countries have admitted women to coholding of the bread basket but without substantially relieving them of holding the laundry basket.

What consequences has industrialization had for age differentiation? Perhaps the most evident change has been in age distribution. The more industrialized a country is, the lower its birth and death rates. These are respectively around 20 and 10 per thousand in "developed" countries, and 40 and 20 per thousand in "developing" countries (euphemistically designating stagnating countries with a galloping demography). Industrial countries have increasingly old populations with far fewer children and far more elderly adults than agrarian countries. In the United States, for example, life expectancy has risen from 49 years in 1900 to 70 years in 1965, while the percentage of the population over 65 years of age grew from 4.0 to 9.6 between 1900 and 1970.

Industrialization has been accompanied also by an enormous expansion of formal educational systems, both in length of training and proportions of the population going through schooling. Mass literacy is only a nineteenth-century phenomenon in the most industrialized countries of Europe, and in Japan; much of Asia, Latin America, and Africa have yet to achieve that goal. Only since the Second World War have substantial proportions of the population in the most industrialized countries attended secondary schools, and only the United States has so far achieved a truly massive system of higher education. The argument is often made that industrial societies require educated labor forces, and to a degree this is true. The skills of the less educated become rapidly obsolete in an advanced industrial country. With automation, there are signs that even the highly educated are in growing oversupply, and that the vast educational machine is overproducing graduates with skills of dubious market value. Increasingly, the schools might have to assume custodial functions (keeping the kids off the streets), as indeed they already do in many working-class, urban neighborhoods.

Rapidly expanding productivity, automation, and the accelerating pace of technological change have all had a marked impact on age differentiation. Increasing leisure is achieved both through shorter work weeks and through fewer years of work.[2] Lengthy training means later entry into a productive activity, and skill obsolescence puts a growing premium on earlier retirement. In the academic professions (medicine, law, university teaching), one typically begins one's career in the late twenties or early thirties, and, in less skilled occupations, a growing number of public service and industrial jobs make employees eligible for a pension after twenty or thirty years of service.

The disparagement of the elderly is perhaps the most striking effect of industrialization on age status. This phenomenon is well-developed in the United States, but present in other countries as well. Compared to agrarian societies, in which the old typically gain in prestige what they lose in strength and power, growing old has few compensations in industrial societies. Of all the types of kinship structure, the nuclear family makes the old most useless and isolated, a condition aggravated by longevity, when older adults survive the departure from home of their youngest child by thirty years or more, and when long periods of widowhood are common.[3]

---

[2] Wilensky (1961, 1966) has argued that the increase in leisure achieved in industrial societies is substantial only if one takes as one's comparison early industrialization in the nineteenth century. He claims that if one takes into account "moonlighting," the increasing proportion of women who enter the labor force, the long hours worked by the professional and managerial elite, and the time spent by women in housework, the amount of time spent working has not substantially declined during the last several decades. It might be argued also that a partial reversal of the respective positions of the "working class" and "leisure class" is taking place: automation is moving highly industrialized societies in the direction of a highly skilled, highly paid, hard working, technocratic, intellectual and managerial elite, and a growing mass of redundant unemployables kept in involuntary indigent indolence.

[3] A common theme in the recent gerontological literature is that the elderly in industrial societies are not really as isolated from their families and societies as they are made out to be (Townsend, 1957; Shanas, 1971). The trouble with studies of this type is that actual situations are compared not with

The extent to which the elderly are cast out and physically segregated is not unique to the United States; it is found in Sweden also. But while in Sweden the old enjoy a nearly all-encompassing social security system, roughly one-fourth of the 20 million Americans over 65 years of age live in indigence and without adequate medical care. The elderly in America are one of the great redundant underclasses created by industrial capitalism. Nearly all adults, with the exception of the "independently wealthy," experience a sharp reduction of their income after retirement. Compared to a median U.S. family income of $9,433 in 1969, those families headed by a person over 65 years of age earned only $4,803, making the penalty for age practically the same as that for being female ($4,821 income for a family with a female head). The median income for families with heads aged 45 to 64 years was $10,808, or well over twice as much as the families headed by an elderly person. In a society that stresses so heavily earning power in the job as a standard of social worth, retirement, especially for men, means loss of status as well as unaccustomed enforced idleness, social isolation, and often poverty or near poverty.

The relative atrophy of an extended family system is undoubtedly the main factor creating both the isolation and the economic plight of the elderly in America. Among other things, the extended family is a small-scale social security system that equalizes wealth among age groups. To the extent that the nuclear family predominates, the elderly not only lose the benefit of sharing the higher income of their younger, economically active, relatives, but they also incur the additional expense of maintaining a separate household. Of course, there are millions of extended families in the United States, and many elderly people are well-integrated within them, but the extended family's elaborately institutionalized kin roles for the elders are not

---

other actual situations in nonindustrial societies, but with inferred "common sense" beliefs about the state of affairs in the other societies. With a standard of comparison this slippery, the facts can be "proved" to be at variance with *any* set of inferred beliefs. Some authors have pointed out correctly that subjective feelings of loneliness among the old and an objective condition of isolation vary independently (Townsend, 1957), and others have suggested that growing old is a mutual process of disengagement of the elderly from society and vice versa (Cumming and Henry, 1961). Such research suffers from the lack of a comparative perspective. So long as we compare empirical conditions with someone else's opinions instead of with other empirical conditions in different times and places, what we say may be true but is unprovable and of extremely limited significance.

the norm, and thus many older people become "socially disengaged," to use a euphemism coined by gerontologists (Cumming & Henry, 1961). Entire industries, not to mention rackets and confidence games, have sprung up in organized attempts to combat or exploit loneliness, isolation, and low income among the elderly.[4] For the few wealthy "senior citizens," "social disengagement" takes the form of luxury cruise ships and air-conditioned, seaside condominiums with community golf courses. At the other (and far more common) extreme of the economic spectrum are the mobile home parks and motels, the dingy rooming houses and transient hotels, and the dilapidated marginal farmsteads long abandoned by those younger. Most of the elderly are not social recluses, but a good many are through no choice of their own, and few are as economically stable as the average middle-aged person.

The segregation of the elderly in the United States is of sufficient magnitude to affect appreciably the age pyramid of entire regions or states. California and Florida, because of their mild climates, have long been magnets for "retirement communities," but just as the more affluent aged move out to await death under sunny climes, the poorer aged stay behind in rural backwaters deserted by the young, but where the cost of living is lower. Although persons over sixty-five account for just under 10 percent of the total population, they make up over 17 percent of the population of sizable areas of Kansas, Nebraska, Iowa, Missouri, Oklahoma, and Texas.

---

[4]The ghettoization of the old, like other forms of social segregation, has given rise to a social science literature justifying these practices as being in the best interests of the aged (Rosow, 1967; Shanas, 1971). As Shanas states, ". . . the aged, like other groups, tend to form friendships with their peers. . . . Old people do better in age-segregated housing" (1971). This line of argument has been used by white and more recently by black segregationists to defend racial segregation. Here, too, the dominance of the conservative strain in Western social science is evident. This bias becomes even more blatant when research is "policy oriented." In the last analysis, what is "policy" if not an attempt to solve at minimum cost what the group in power perceives as "social problems"? Interestingly, the locus of the problem is most often perceived as being in the powerless groups: "the Jewish problem," "the Negro problem," "the youth problem," "the hippie problem," "the criminal problem," and so on. If the reader objects that the perspective adopted in this book is equally facile, I shall agree with him, but until it becomes the new orthodoxy, it should at least prove more provocative.

Being old in industrial societies has different effects on men and women. Women not only live longer than men, but the *gap* in longevity between men and women has widened as life expectancy has risen. In 1900, males could be expected to reach on the average the age of 48, and women, 51, a difference of 3 years; by 1965, life expectancy for males had reached 67, and for females, 74, a 7-year gap. This naturally means that an increasing proportion of older people are women. There are only about 75 American men over 65 for every 100 women in the same age group. This, in turn, has a profound influence on marital status, further accentuated by the fact that wives are on the average younger than husbands. Only 29 percent of American males over 65 are unmarried, compared to 62 percent of females.

Gerontologists seem to agree that being married is probably the single most important factor mitigating the predicament of old age in industrial societies. Happily married old couples (and there seem to be relatively more of them than happily married young couples) rely on each other for companionship more exclusively than younger couples, and seem to develop a more sex-egalitarian relationship than prevailed during middle age (Clark & Anderson, 1967). This greater gender equality appears to be the result of a gradual breakdown in sex-role boundaries and increased flexibility in the domestic division of labor by gender after the husband retires and spends much of his time at home. Perhaps this breakdown in the sexual division of labor results from the man's having lost his male role of provider, and the woman's having lost her role of child raiser. The significant fact, however, is that because of their greater longevity and difficulty in remarrying, many more older women than men spend their last years single.

Not only are women considered to lose their youth, sexual attractiveness, and social worth much sooner than men, but a "favorable" sex ratio in old age condemns them to greater social isolation than their male counterparts. As is often the case, social stigmas are cumulative. The old woman suffers under the double jeopardy of age and sex, much as the black woman must pay the double penalty of race and sex. Given the economic destitution and the poor health that plague so many of the old, the greater longevity of women is indeed a mixed blessing.

Although its effects are most severe on the old, age segregation is not limited to the elderly in industrial societies. Both schooling and military service are age-grading and age-segregating institutions that affect large sections of the population. The young are at least as segregated as the elderly, since the emphasis on age peer pressures and conformity is strongest during the "teen" years. Adolescent and youth "cultures," although not unique to industrial societies, are probably more differentiated there than in most preindustrial societies, with the possible exception of some of the age-graded

African societies discussed earlier. Margaret Mead (1953) has demonstrated that the behavior syndrome of awkwardness, insecurity, and irresponsibility associated with adolescence in Western societies is mainly, if not exclusively, culturally determined. In few societies are the young expected to go through a "crisis" during which they express ritualized forms of revolt against "adult culture."

The "youth movement" so extensively written about during the last few years is partly an extension to a slightly older age group of this long-standing phenomenon. Adolescence has been extended into the twenties (as indeed has the period of formal training and education during which youth segregation is at a maximum), and, as the term *movement* implies, the ritualized rebellion of youth has become more self-consciously ideologized in both political and cultural dimensions. For all its vicarious identification with the poor, the blacks, and other oppressed groups, there is little evidence that the youth movement is more than ritualized age conflict channeled into political rhetoric and "alternate life styles." The youth movement affects mostly the college population, that is, a predominantly middle-class group affluent enough to afford the luxuries of extended schooling and economically parasitic "rebellion." Much of their pseudo-radicalism vanishes upon the assumption of full adult status, which comes with job taking, marriage, and parenthood. As for the specific cultural forms that the youth movement takes, they are more symptomatic of a decadent than of a revolutionary society.

Evidence suggests that the relationship between sex status and age in the American family is curvilinear: the inequality between husband and wife is greater during the middle years, especially during the child-rearing stage, than either during the early or the late years of marriage (Safilios-Rothschild, 1972). The general pattern seems to be that as young couples have children, the greater egalitarianism of early marriage yields to a more sharply differentiated division of labor by sex, with the attendant domestication of women and casting of men in the provider role. After children leave the parental "nest" to establish their own nuclear families, the reentry of the wife into the labor force, and/or the retirement of the man seem to reverse the trend back toward the greater equality of their earlier years.

This complex relationship between age and sex status is probably accountable for by two factors. The first reason is general to human societies, namely, that infant dependency has tied women to the home, probably from the dawn of human evolution. The second is more specific to American society, or, at least, to capitalist societies. Sex status in America is closely linked with contribution to the family's monetary income. This is merely a special case of money as an important determinant of general status. When pecuniary evaluation is strongly stressed, and when household work is not remunerated in cash, the "mere housewife" is in a lower occupational status than the "gainfully employed" woman. The low status of housewife is thus linked to both sex and occupation.

Industrialization and its correlates (urbanization, complex division of labor, geographical mobility, and so on) have affected both age and sex differentiation, but they have not come even close to eliminating their social significance nor the inequality between age and sex groups. In terms of age, industrialization has probably brought about a higher rate of skill obsolescence, a lengthier period of formal schooling, a shortening of the economically productive life-span, greater longevity, a slight rejuvenation of the age class in power compared to agrarian societies, a rigidly age-stratified educational system, some reduction in the importance of age as a dimension of adult status relative to class, ethnicity, race, and other characteristics, and decreased status for persons beyond the economically active age.

Regarding sex, industrialization (and its attendant political revolutions) has appreciably increased the legal position of women in civic rights, and property and family law, but it has not appreciably reduced the actual amount of male political dominance. In the economic sphere, women in industrial societies have a much wider range of occupations to choose from than they did in agrarian societies; but so do men, of course. The amount of occupational gender segregation in most industrial societies has remained fairly constant, and as is almost invariably the case, the segregation has been heavily detrimental to the politically subordinate group. Sex discrimination is the most widespread and blatant form of ascriptive discrimination in all industrial societies with the exception of South Africa, where racism takes first place. Even in as racist a society as the United States, discrimination on the basis of sex far outweighs racial discrimination as a source of differences in earnings. Certainly, the *potential* for emancipation from the physiological constraints of sexual dimorphism (made possible by industrialization) has not come anywhere near realization in most industrial societies.

Ideology, however, does seem to make a difference, and much more so in relation to sex than in relation to age. It is difficult to conceive of any society in which the staggering advantage of adults over children in strength, knowledge, and experience could ever be overcome. Industrial societies reduce the significance of brute strength and perhaps of experience to some extent, but greatly increase the weight of technical knowledge. The United States has probably gone further than any other industrial society in idealizing youth, but a youth cult does not any more a "juvenocracy" make than the Medieval European cult of women (chivalry, romantic love) made that society a matriarchy. The status of women has, however, been markedly affected by the great revolutionary movements during the last two centuries. The French and other bourgeois revolutions of the nineteenth century were directly linked to the changes in legal institutions, leading first to the abolition of slavery, and later to the enfranchisement of women in the bourgeois democracies. The Bolshevik, Chinese, and similar socialist revolutions of the twentieth century marked another important qualitative jump in women's status, a jump stimulated in good part by changes in family structure and the collectivization of production on a crash and largely coercive basis. The massive, organized, and compulsory effort to maximize production and to industrialize in the shortest possible time obviously entailed efficiently tapping the vast, underutilized reservoir of womanpower. This, in turn, called for the collectivization of infant rearing. Equality between the sexes, though still far from completely realized, is nevertheless one of the greatest achievements of the socialist countries. The price, of course, was a substantial loss of personal freedom to great numbers of both men and women, but such, it seems, is the price of any far reaching revolution.

There is a basic contradiction between freedom and equality. The bourgeois democracies achieved a considerable measure of individual freedom at the cost of perpetuating numerous forms of inequality. The freedom guaranteed by the legal institutions of bourgeois democracies has remained, in effect, a privilege of class, sex, and race. The nineteenth-century revolutions were clearly freedom-fostering movements, the benefits of which were very unequally distributed. The twentieth century saw the advent of "equality revolutions" that, in order to bring about greater equity in the distribution of scarce resources among individuals and groups, had to resort to massive coercion, thereby ironically creating new types of tyrannical oligarchies. In the words of George Orwell, the brilliant fabalist of modern tyranny, "all animals are equal, but some are more equal than others." At least a few societies have demonstrated that the more equal ones need not necessarily be male. None has yet demonstrated that big animals are not necessarily more equal than small ones.

Glossary

Age grade: A position in an age hierarchy, for example, the "Freshman class" in a college.
Age set: A group of people or cohort who move up together through an *age-grade* system.
Apes: The living primate species most closely related to man, including gibbons, orangutans, gorillas, and chimpanzees (Lat.: *Pongidae*).
Bilateral descent: A system of tracing descent that gives all of a person's ancestors equal or nearly equal social significance.
Biogram: The inherited behavioral repertoire of a species.
Clan: In a *unilineal descent* society, a group of people who, rightly or wrongly, claim descent from a single ancestor.
Endogamy: A rule of marriage that enjoins or encourages marriage *within* a given group.
Environmentalism: In the social sciences, those theories that stressed the importance of the milieu, and especially the social milieu in determining human behavior.
Ethnocentrism: The judgment of another culture by the norms of one's own. The opposite of cultural relativism.
Eugenics: The theory and practice of improving the genetic stock, usually applied to humans, as in sterilization of the insane.
Exogamy: A rule of marriage that prescribes or encourages marriage *outside* a given group.
Extended family: A group of persons living together and related by blood or marriage, which includes individuals other than a married couple and their unmarried offspring.
Functionalism: In the social sciences, the theory that societies are made up of interdependent and specialized parts which contribute to the maintenance of the whole.
Genotype: The genetic composition of an organism, as distinguished from its outward appearance or *phenotype*.
Gerontocracy: Government by the older.

Glossary

Hermaphroditism: A condition wherein a single organism normally carries the gametes (sex cells) or sex organs for both sexes. By extension, any of a number of anomalies that make the gender of an individual phenotypically ambiguous.

Hypergamy: A form of marriage wherein a woman marries a husband of higher social status than her own.

Imprinting: A type of behavior established in the young of a species in response to specific stimuli during a limited and critical period in the organism's maturation, and difficult to extinguish once established.

Intraspecific: Within a single biological species. The opposite of *interspecific*, or between species.

Lineage: In a system of *unilineal descent*, a group of people who can trace their descent to a common ancestor.

Matrilineal descent: A system of tracing descent through a person's mother, mother's mother, mother's mother's mother, and so on.

Morphology: In biology, the science of the structure of organisms.

Neolocal residence: A rule or preference whereby, upon marriage, bride and groom establish a new, separate household.

Nuclear family: A family group consisting only of husband, wife, and their unmarried offspring.

Patrilineal descent: A system of tracing descent through a person's father, father's father, father's father's father, and so on.

Phenotype: The outward appearance of an organism, as distinguished from its genetic composition or *genotype*.

Phylogenesis: The evolutionary development of a species.

Physiology: In biology, the science of the functioning of organisms.

Polyandry: A rare form of marriage whereby a woman is simultaneously married to several husbands.

Polygamy: A form of marriage wherein an individual of either sex is simultaneously married to several individuals of the opposite sex. Polygamy can take the rare form of *polyandry* or the common form of *polygyny*.

Polygyny: A common form of marriage wherein a man is simultaneously married to several wives.

Primates: An order of mammals made up of approximately 190 living species, including *Homo sapiens*, the apes, the Old and New World monkeys, and the lower primates.

Primogeniture: A rule whereby inheritance of power, status, and/or wealth is passed on from father to eldest son.

Relativism: A theory, first developed in anthropology, that every culture must be understood and evaluated in its own terms, and not by applying to it criteria of another culture (typically one's own). The opposite of ethnocentrism.

Sexual dimorphism: The morphological (size, shape) differences in secondary sexual characteristics existing between the males and females of the same species.

Unilineal descent: A system of tracing descent that emphasizes one single line of ancestors, either males or females.

Unilinear evolutionism: A widely held theory in nineteenth-century social science that human societies could be ordered on a single evolutionary continuum, from the primitive to the advanced. This was frequently presented in the form of stages of culture such as savagery, barbarism, and civilization.

Uxorilocal residence: A rule or preference whereby, upon marriage, the groom comes to live with his bride and her relatives. Also called *matrilocal residence.*

Virilocal residence: A rule or preference whereby, upon marriage, the bride comes to live with her husband and his relatives. Also called *patrilocal residence.*

Bibliography

Aberle, D. F., *et al.* "The Incest Taboo and the Mating Patterns of Animals." *American Anthropologist*, 65:253-66, 1963.
Acsádi, György, and Nemeskéri, J. *History of Human Life Span and Mortality.* Budapest: Akadémiai Kiadó, 1970.
Altmann, Stuart A. *Social Communication among Primates.* Chicago: University of Chicago Press, 1967.
⎯⎯⎯, and Altmann, Jeanne. *Baboon Ecology.* Chicago: University of Chicago Press, 1970.
Ardrey, Robert. *African Genesis.* New York: Atheneum, 1961.
⎯⎯⎯. *The Territorial Imperative.* New York: Atheneum, 1966.
Aronson, Lester R.; Tobach, Ethel; Lehrman, Daniel S.; and Rosenblatt, Jay S., eds. *Development and Evolution of Behavior.* San Francisco: W. H. Freeman, 1970.
Astin, Helen S. *The Woman Doctorate in America.* New York: Russell Sage Foundation, 1969.
Bardwick, Judith M. *Psychology of Women.* New York: Harper & Row, 1971.
Barron, Milton L. *The Aging American: An Introduction to Social Gerontology and Geriatrics.* New York: Thomas Y. Crowell, 1961.
Barry, H.; Bacon, Margaret K.; and Child, I. I. "A Cross-Cultural Survey of Some Sex Differences in Socialization." *Journal of Abnormal and Social Psychology*, 55:327-32, 1957.
Bart, Pauline B. "Sexism and Social Science." *Journal of Marriage and the Family*, 33(4):734-45, 1971.
Bascom, William. *The Yoruba of Southwestern Nigeria.* New York: Holt, Rinehart and Winston, 1970.
Beach, Frank A., ed. *Sex and Behavior.* New York: John Wiley & Sons, 1965.

Bibliography

Bebel, August. *Die Frau und der Socialismus*. Berlin: Dietz, 1923.
Benedict, Ruth. "Continuities and Discontinuities in Cultural Conditioning." *Psychiatry*, 1:161-67, 1938.
Bernardi, B. "The Age-System of the Masai." *Annali Lateranensi* (Città del Vaticano), 18:257-318, 1955.
Birren, James E. *The Psychology of Aging*. Englewood Cliffs, N.J.: Prentice-Hall, 1964.
Booth, Alan. "Sex and Social Partipication." *American Sociological Review*, 37(2):183-93, 1972.
Bowlby, John. *Attachment*. New York: Basic Books, 1969.
Briggs, L. Cabot. *The Living Races of the Sahara Desert*. Cambridge, Mass.: Peabody Museum, 1958.
Brown, Judith K. "A Note on the Division of Labor by Sex." *American Anthropologist*, 72:1073-78, 1970.
Buettner-Janush, John. *Origins of Man, Physical Anthropology*. New York: John Wiley & Sons, 1966.
Burgess, Ernest W., ed. *Aging in Western Societies*. Chicago: University of Chicago Pres, 1959.
Cannon, Walter B. *The Wisdom of the Body*. New York: W. W. Norton, 1932.
Carpenter, C. R. "A Field Study in Siam of the Behavior and Social Relations of the Gibbon." *Comparative Psychological Monographs*, 16:1-212, 1940.
Chance, Michael R. A., and Jolly, Clifford J. *Social Groups of Monkeys, Apes and Men*. London: Jonathan Cape, 1970.
Chapple, Eliot Dismore. *Culture and Biological Man*. New York: Holt, Rinehart and Winston, 1970.
Clark, Margaret, and Anderson, Barbara. *Culture and Aging*. Springfield, Ill.: Charles C Thomas, 1967.
Clignet, Rémi. *Many Wives, Many Powers*. Evanston, Ill.: Northwestern University Press, 1970.
Cohen, Abner. *Custom and Politics in Urban Africa*. Berkeley: University of California Press, 1969.
Collins, Randall. "A Conflict Theory of Sexual Stratification." *Social Problems*, 19(1):3-21, 1971.
Comfort, Alex. *Aging, the Biology of Senescence*. New York: Holt, Rinehart and Winston, 1964.
Comhaire-Sylvain, Suzanne. *Femmes de Kinshasa*. Paris: Mouton, 1968.
Count, E. W. "The Biological Basis of Human Sociality." *American Anthropologist*, 60:1049-85, 1958.
Crook, J. H., and Gartlan, J. S. "Evolution of Primate Societies." *Nature*, 210:1200-3, 1966.
Cumming, Elaine, and Henry, William E. *Growing Old: The Process of Disengagement*. New York: Basic Books, 1961.
D'Andrade, Roy G. "Sex Differences and Cultural Institutions." *The Development of Sex Differences*, Edited by Eleanor E. Maccoby. Stanford: Stanford University Press, 1966.

Bibliography

Davenport, William. "Sexual Patterns and Their Regulation in a Society of the Southwest Pacific." *Sex and Behavior*. Edited by Frank A. Beach. New York: John Wiley & Sons, 1965.
de Beauvoir, Simone. *The Second Sex*. New York: Alfred A. Knopf, 1952.
de Groot, J. "The Influence of Limbic Structures on Pituitary Functions Related to Reproduction." *Sex and Behavior*. Edited by Frank A. Beach. New York: John Wiley & Sons, 1965.
Denham, Woodrow W. "Nonhuman Primate Behavior: A Note on Recent Research." *American Anthropologist*, 72:365-67, 1970.
De Vore, Irven. "The Social Behavior and Organization of Baboon Troops." Ph.D. dissertation, University of Chicago, 1962.
_____. "Male Dominance and Mating Behavior in Baboons." *Sex and Behavior*. Edited by Frank A. Beach. New York: John Wiley & Sons, 1965.
_____, ed. *Primate Behavior*. New York: Holt, Rinehart and Winston, 1965.
_____, and Washburn, S. L. "Baboon Ecology and Human Evolution." *Viking Press Publications in Anthropology*, 36:335-367, 1963.
Diamond, M. "A Critical Evaluation of the Ontogeny of Human Sexual Behavior." *Quarterly Review of Biology*, 40:147-75, 1965.
Downie, D. C., and Hally, D. J. "A Cross-Cultural Study of Male Transvestism and Sex-Role Differentiation. Unpublished MS, Dartmouth College, Hanover, N.H., 1961.
Eisenstadt, S. N. *From Generation to Generation*. Glencoe, Ill.: The Free Press, 1956.
_____. *Essays on Comparative Institutions*. New York: John Wiley & Sons, 1965.
Ellefson, J. O. "Territorial Behavior in the Common White-Handed Gibbon." *Primates*. Edited by P. C. Jay. New York: Holt, Rinehart and Winston, 1963.
Ember, Melvin, and Ember, Carol R. "The Conditions Favoring Matrilocal versus Patrilocal Residence." *American Anthropologist*, 73(3):571-94, 1971.
Engels, Friedrich. *The Origin of the Family, Private Property and the State*. New York: International Publishers, 1942.
Epstein, Cynthia. *Woman's Place*. Berkeley: University of California Press, 1970.
Evans-Pritchard, E. E. *The Position of Women in Primitive Societies*. New York: The Free Press, 1965.
_____. "Sexual Inversion among the Azande." *American Anthropologist*, 72:1428-34, 1970.
Firestone, Shulamith. *The Dialectic of Sex*. New York: Bantam Books, 1970.

Bibliography

Ford, C. S., and Beach. F. *Patterns of Sexual Behavior*. New York: Harper & Row, 1951.
Fox, Robin. "In the Beginning: Aspects of Hominid Behavioural Evolution." *Man*, 2:415-33, 1967a.
―――. *Kinship and Marriage*. London: Pelican Books, 1967b.
Frazier, E. Franklin. *The Negro Family in the United States*. New York: Citadel, 1948.
Fried, Morton; Harris, Marvin; and Murphy, Robert, eds. *War: The Anthropology of Armed Conflict and Aggression*. Garden City, N.Y.: Natural History Press, 1968.
Friedan, Betty. *The Feminine Mystique*. New York: Dell, 1963.
Friedenberg, Edgar Z. *Coming of Age in America*. New York: Random House, 1965.
Frisch, J. "Individual Behavior and Intertroop Variability in Japanese Macaques." *Primates*. Edited by P. Jay. New York: Holt, Rinehart and Winston, 1968.
Fromm, Eric. "Sex and Character." *Psychiatry*, 6(1):21-41, 1943.
Garattini, S., and Sigg, E. B., eds. *Aggressive Behavior*. New York: John Wiley & Sons, 1969.
Gartlan, J. S. "Structure and Function in Primate Society." *Folia Primatologia*, 8:89-120, 1968.
Gibbs, James L., ed. *Peoples of Africa*. New York: Holt, Rinehart and Winston, 1965.
Gluckman, Max. *Rituals of Rebellion in South East Africa*. Manchester: Manchester University Press, 1954.
―――. *Custom and Conflict in Africa*. Oxford: Blackwell, 1955.
Goode, William J., *World Revolution and Family Patterns*. New York: The Free Press, 1963.
―――. "Force and Violence in the Family." *Journal of Marriage and the Family*, 33(4):624-36, 1971.
Gough, Kathleen. "The Origin of the Family." *Journal of Marriage and the Family*, 33(4):760-70, 1971.
Gouldner, A. W., and Peterson, R. A. *Notes on Technology and the Moral Order*. Indianapolis: Bobbs-Merrill, 1963.
Gross, Edward. "Plus ça Change ... ? The Sexual Structure of Occupations over Time." *Social Problems*, 16(2):198-208, 1968.
―――. Private communication, 1972.
Hacker, H. M. "Women as a Minority Group." *Social Forces*, 30(1):60-68, 1951.
Hamburg, David A., and Lunde, Donald T. "Sex Hormones in the Development of Sex Differences in Human Behavior." *The Development of Sex Differences*. Edited by Eleanor E. Maccoby. Stanford: Stanford University Press, 1966.
Hampson, John L. "Determinants of Psychosexual Orientation." *Sex and Behavior*. Edited by Frank A. Beach. New York: John Wiley & Sons, 1965.

Harlow, Harry F. "Basic Social Capacity of Primates." *Human Biology*, 31:40-53, 1959.
⎯⎯⎯⎯. "The Heterosexual Affectional System in Monkeys." *American Psychologist*, 17:1-9, 1962.
⎯⎯⎯⎯. "Sexual Behavior in the Rhesus Monkey." *Sex and Behavior*. Edited by Frank A. Beach. New York: John Wiley & Sons, 1965.
⎯⎯⎯⎯, and Harlow, Margaret K. "The Effect of Rearing Conditions on Behavior." *Sex Research: New Developments*. Edited by John Money. New York: Holt, Rinehart and Winston, 1965.
Harrison, G. A.; Weiner, J. S.; Tanner, J. M.; and Barnicot, N. A. *Human Biology, An Introduction to Human Evolution*. New York: Oxford University Press, 1964.
Hobbs, Lisa. *Love and Liberation*. New York: McGraw-Hill, 1970.
Hole, Judith, and Levine, Ellen. *Rebirth of Feminism*. New York: Quadrangle Books, 1971.
Holter, Harriet. *Sex Roles and Social Structure*. Oslo: Universitetsforlaget, 1970.
⎯⎯⎯⎯. "Sex Roles and Social Change." *Acta Sociologica*, 14(1-2):2-12, 1971.
Homans, George C., and Schneider, David. *Marriage Authority and Final Causes*. Glencoe, Ill.: The Free Press, 1955.
Horney, Karen. *Feminine Psychology*. New York: W. W. Norton, 1967.
Howe, Irving. "The Middle-Class Mind of Kate Millet." *Harper's*, December, 1970, pp. 110-29.
Hymes, Dell H. *Language in Culture and Society*. New York: Harper & Row, 1964.
Jacob, André, ed. *Points de Vue sur le Langage*. Paris: Klincksieck, 1969.
Janeway, Elizabeth. *Man's World, Woman's Place*. New York: William Morrow, 1971.
Jay, Phyllis C., ed. *Primates*. New York: Holt, Rinehart and Winston, 1968.
Jensen, Arthur. "How Much Can We Boost IQ and Scholastic Achievement?" *Harvard Educational Review*, Reprint Series, No. 2, 1969.
Kagan, Jerome. *Birth to Maturity, A Study in Psychological Development*. New York: John Wiley & Sons, 1962.
⎯⎯⎯⎯. *Change and Continuity in Infancy*. New York: John Wiley & Sons, 1971.
Kawai, Masao, and Mizuhara, Kiroki. "An Ecological Study on the Wild Mountain Gorilla." *Primates*, 2(1):1-42, 1959.
Kawamura, S. "The Process of Sub-Culture Propagation among Japanese Macaques." *Primate Social Behavior*. Edited by C. H. Southwick. Princeton, N.J.: D. Van Nostrand, 1963.
Kinsey, A. C.; Martin, C. E.; and Pomeroy, W. B. *Sexual Response in the Human Male*. Philadelphia and London: W. B. Saunders, 1948.

Bibliography

Kinsey, A. C.; Pomeroy, W. B.; Martin, C. E.; and Gebhard, D. H. *Sexual Behavior in the Human Female*. Philadelphia and London: W. B. Saunders, 1953.

Kephart, William M. *The Family, Society and the Individual*. Boston: Houghton Mifflin, 1966.

Kohlberg, Lawrence. "A Cognitive-Developmental Analysis of Children's Sex-Role Concepts and Attitudes." *The Development of Sex Differences*. Edited by Eleanor E. Maccoby. Stanford: Stanford University Press, 1966.

Koller, Marvin R. *Social Gerontology*. New York: Random House, 1968.

Kortlandt, Adriaan. "Chimpanzees in the Wild." *Scientific American*, 206:128-38, 1962.

Klopfer, Peter H. "From Ardrey to Altruism: A Discourse on the Biological Basis of Human Behavior." *Behavioral Science*, 13:399-401, 1968.

Kummer, Hans. *Social Organization of Hamadryas Baboons*. Chicago: University of Chicago Press, 1968.

_____. *Primate Societies*. Chicago: Aldine-Atherton, 1971.

La Barre, W. *The Human Animal*. Chicago: University of Chicago Press, 1954.

Landar, Herbert Jay. *Language and Culture*. New York: Oxford University Press, 1966.

Lehrman, Daniel S. "Semantic and Conceptual Issues in the Nature-Nurture Problem." *Development and Evolution of Behavior*. Edited by Lester R. Aronson *et al*. San Francisco: W. H. Freeman, 1970.

Lenin, Vladimir Ilich. *Women and Society*. New York: International Publishers, 1938.

Lenneberg, Eric H. *Biological Foundations of Language*. New York: John Wiley & Sons, 1967.

Lévi-Strauss, Claude. *The Elementary Structures of Kinship*. Boston: Beacon Press, 1968.

Lifton, Robert Jay, ed. *The Woman in America*. Cambridge, Mass.: Houghton Mifflin, 1965.

Lhote, Henri. *Les Touaregs de Hoggar*. Paris: Payot, 1944.

Linton, Ralph. "Age and Sex Categories." *American Sociological Review*, 7:589-603, 1942.

Lloyd, Peter C. "The Yoruba of Nigeria." *Peoples of Africa*. Edited by James L. Gibbs. New York: Holt, Rinehart and Winston, 1965.

Loether, Herman John. *Problems of Aging*. Belmont, Calif.: Dickenson, 1967.

Lorenz, Konrad Z. *Evolution and Modification of Behavior*. Chicago: University of Chicago Press, 1965.

_____. *On Aggression*. New York: Harcourt, Brace and World, 1966.

_____. *Studies in Animal and Human Behavior*. Cambridge, Mass.: Harvard University Press, 1970.

Maccoby, Eleanor, ed. *The Development of Sex Differences*. Stanford: Stanford University Press, 1966.
Maclean, Paul D. "New Findings Relevant to the Evolution of Psychosexual Functions of the Brain." *Sex Research, New Developments*. Edited by John Money. New York: Holt, Rinehart and Winston, 1965.
Malinowski, Bronislaw. *Sex and Repression in Savage Society*. London: Paul, Trench and Trubner, 1927.
_____. *The Sexual Life of Savages*. London: Routledge, 1929.
Marx, Karl. *The Holy Family*. Moscow: Foreign Language Publishing House, 1956.
_____; Engels, Friedrich; and Stalin, Joseph. *Women and Communism*. London: Lawrence and Wishart, 1950.
Mason, William A. "Field and Laboratory Studies of Social Organization in *Saimiri* and *Callicebus*." *Primate Behavior*, II. Edited by Leonard A. Rosenblum. New York: Academic Press, 1971.
Masters, William H., and Johnson, Virginia E. "The Sexual Response Cycles of the Human Male and Female." *Sex and Behavior*. Edited by Frank A. Beach. New York: John Wiley & Sons, 1965.
_____. *Human Sexual Response*. Boston: Little, Brown, 1966.
Mead, Margaret. *Sex and Temperament*. New York: Morrow, 1935.
_____. *Male and Female*. New York: Morrow, 1949.
_____. *The Coming of Age in Samoa*. New York: Modern Library, 1953.
Mill, John Stuart. *The Subjection of Women*. London: Longmans, 1869.
Miller, Robert E. "Experimental Studies of Communication in the Monkey." *Primate Behavior*, II. Edited by Leonard A. Rosenblum. New York: Academic Press, 1971.
Millett, Kate. *Sexual Politics*. New York: Doubleday, 1970.
Mischel, Walter. "A Social Learning View of Sex Differences in Behavior." *The Development of Sex Differences*. Edited by Eleanor E. Maccoby. Stanford: Stanford University Press, 1966.
Mitchell, Juliet. "The Longest Revolution." *Masculine-Feminine*. Edited by Betty Roszak and Theodore Roszak. New York: Harper & Row, 1969.
_____. *Woman's Estate*. New York: Random House, 1972.
Money, John, ed. *Sex Research, New Developments*. New York: Holt, Rinehart and Winston, 1965.
Montagu, Ashley. *The Natural Superiority of Women*. New York: Macmillan, 1968.
_____. *Sex, Man and Society*. New York: G. P. Putnam's Sons, 1969.
Morgan, Elaine. *The Descent of Woman*. London: Souvenir Press, 1972.

Bibliography

Morgan, Lewis Henry. *Ancient Society*. New York: Henry Holt, 1877.
Morgan, Robin, ed. *Sisterhood Is Powerful*. New York: Random House, 1970.
Morris, Desmond. *Primate Ethology*. London: Weidenfeld and Nicolson, 1967a.
────. *The Naked Ape*. London: Jonathan Cape, 1967b.
Morris, Ramona, and Morris, Desmond. *Men and Apes*. New York: McGraw-Hill, 1966.
Munroe, Robert L.; Whiting, John W. M.; and Hally, David J. "Institutionalized Male Transvestism and Sex Distinctions." *American Anthropologist*, 71:87-91, 1969.
Murdock, G. P. "Comparative Data on the Division of Labor by Sex." *Social Forces*, 15:551-53, 1935.
────. *Social Structure*. New York: Macmillan, 1949.
────. "World Ethnographic Sample." *American Anthropologist*, 59:664-87, 1957.
Murphy, Robert Francis. *The Dialectics of Social Life*. New York: Basic Books, 1971.
Muuss, Rolf E. H. *Theories of Adolescence*. New York: Random House, 1968.
Napier, John. *The Roots of Mankind*. Washington, D.C.: Smithsonian Institution Press, 1970.
────, and Napier, P. H. *Handbook of Living Primates*. New York: Academic Press, 1967.
National Geographic Society. *Monkeys, Apes and Man*. Film. Washington, D.C., 1971.
Norbeck, Edward. "African Rituals of Rebellion." *American Anthropologist*, 65:1254-79, 1963.
Parsons, Talcott. "Age and Sex in the Social Structure of the United States." *American Sociological Review*, 7:604-16, 1942.
────, and Bales, Robert F. *Family, Socialization and Interaction Process*. Glencoe, Ill.: The Free Press, 1954.
Paulme, Denise. *Women of Tropical Africa*. London: Routledge and Kegan Paul, 1963.
Piaget, Jean. *Genetic Epistemology*. New York: Columbia University Press, 1970.
Radcliffe-Brown, Alfred R. *Structure and Function in Primitive Society*. Glencoe, Ill.: The Free Press, 1952.
Read, Kenneth E. *The High Valley*. New York: Charles Scribner's Sons, 1965.
Reynolds, Vernon. *The Apes*. New York: E. P. Dutton, 1967.
Riley, Matilda W. "Social Gerontology and the Age Stratification of Society." *Gerontologist*, 11:79-87, 1971.
────, and Foner, Anne. *Aging and Society*, I. New York: Russell Sage Foundation, 1968.

Bibliography

Riley, Matilda W.; Riley, John W.; and Johnson, Marilyn E. *Aging and Society*, II. New York: Russell Sage Foundaaton, 1969.
Riley, Matilda W.; Johnson, Marilyn E.; and Foner, Anne. *Aging and Society*, III. New York: Russell Sage Foundation, 1972.
Rocheblave-Spenlé, Anne-Marie. *Les Rôles Masculins/Féminins*. Paris: Presses Universitaires de France, 1964.
Rose, Arnold M., and Peterson, Warren A., eds. *Older People and Their Social World*. Philadelphia: F. A. Davis, 1965.
Rosenblum, Leonard A., ed. *Primate Behavior*, II. New York: Academic Press, 1971.
Rosow, Irving. *Social Integration of the Aged*. New York: The Free Press, 1967.
Rossi, Alice S. "Equality between the Sexes: An Immodest Proposal." *The Woman in America*. Edited by Robert Jay Lifton. Cambridge, Mass.: Houghton Mifflin, 1965.
⎯⎯⎯⎯. "Sex Equality, the Beginning of Ideology." *Masculine/Feminine*. Edited by Betty Roszak and Theodore Roszak. New York: Harper & Row, 1969.
Roszak, Betty, and Roszak, Theodore, eds. *Masculine/Feminine*. New York: Harper & Row, 1969.
Rowell, Thelma. "Long-Term Changes in a Population of Uganda Baboons." *Folia Primatologica*, 11(4):241-54, 1969.
Sade, D. S. "Some Aspects of Parent-Offspring and Sibling Relations in a Group of Rhesus Monkeys." *American Journal of Physical Anthropology*, 23:1-18, 1965.
Safilios-Rothschild, Constantina. "A Cross-Cultural Examination of Women's Marital, Educational and Occupational Options." *Acta Sociologica*, 14(1-2):96-113, 1971.
⎯⎯⎯⎯. *Toward a Sociology of Women*. Lexington, Mass.: Xerox College Publishing, 1972.
Schaller, G. B. *The Mountain Gorilla*. Chicago: University of Chicago Press, 1963.
Schneider, David M., and Gough, Kathleen. *Matrilineal Kinship*. Berkeley: University of California Press, 1961.
Schneirla, T. C. "The Interrelationships of the 'Innate' and the 'Acquired' in Instinctive Behavior." *L'Instinct dans le Comportement des Animaux et de l'Homme*. Edited by P. P. Grassé. Paris: Masson, 1956.
Schultz, Adolph H. *The Life of Primates*. New York: Universe Books, 1969.
Schwendinger, Julia, and Schwendinger, Herman. "Sociology's Founding Fathers, Sexists to a Man." *Journal of Marriage and the Family*, 33(4):783-99, 1971.
Sears, Robert R. "Development of Gender Role." *Sex and Behavior*. Edited by Frank A. Beach. New York: John Wiley & Sons, 1965.

Bibliography

Sears, Robert R.; Maccoby, E. E.; and Levin, H. *Patterns of Child Rearing*. Stanford: Stanford University Press, 1957.

Seidman, Jerome M., ed. *The Child, a Book of Readings*. New York: Holt, Rinehart and Winston, 1966.

Service, Elman R. *The Hunters*. Englewood Cliffs, N.J.: Prentice-Hall, 1966.

———. *Cultural Evolutionism*. New York: Holt, Rinehart and Winston, 1971.

Seward, Georgene H., and Williamsen, Robert C., eds. *Sex Roles in Changing Society*. New York: Random House, 1970.

Shanas, Ethel. "The Sociology of Aging and the Aged." *The Sociological Quarterly*, 12:159-76, 1971.

———, and Streib, Gordon F., eds. *Social Structure and the Family, Generational Relations*. Englewood Cliffs, N.J.: Prentice-Hall, 1965.

———, et al. *Older People in Three Industrial Societies*. New York: Aldine-Atherton, 1968.

Shock, Nathan W. *Biological Aspects of Aging*. New York: Columbia University Press, 1962a.

———. "The Physiology of Aging." *Scientific American*, 206:100-10, 1962b.

Simmons, Leo W. *The Role of the Aged in Primitive Society*. New Haven, Conn.: Yale University Press, 1945.

Smith, Mary F. *Baba of Karo, A Woman of the Moslem Hausa*. London: Faber and Faber, 1954.

Smith, M. G. *The Economy of Hausa Communities of Zaria*. London: Her Majesty's Stationery Office, 1955.

———. *Government in Zazzau, 1800-1950*. London: Oxford University Press, 1960.

Southwick, Charles H. *Primate Social Behavior*. Princeton, N.J.: D. Van Nostrand, 1963.

Spiro, M. E. *Kibbutz: Venture in Utopia*. Cambridge, Mass.: Harvard University Press, 1956.

———. *Children of the Kibbutz*. Cambridge, Mass.: Harvard University Press, 1958.

Spuhler, James N. *Genetic Diversity and Human Behavior*. Chicago: Aldine-Atherton, 1967.

Starck, D.; Schneider, R.; and Kuhn, H. J., eds. *Progress in Primatology*. Stuttgart: Gustav Fischer, 1967.

Stebbins, George L. *Processes of Organic Evolution*. Englewood Cliffs, N.J.: Prentice-Hall, 1966.

———. *The Basis of Progressive Evolution*. Chapel Hill: University of North Carolina Press, 1969.

Stephens, William N. *The Family in Cross-Cultural Perspective*. New York: Holt, Rinehart and Winston, 1963.

Talland, George A., ed. *Human Aging and Behavior*. New York: Academic Press, 1968.

Tanner, James Mourilyan. *Human Growth*. Oxford: Pergamon, 1960.
———. *Growth at Adolescence*. Oxford: Blackwell, 1962.
Tibbitts, Clark, ed. *Handbook of Social Gerontology*. Chicago: University of Chicago Press, 1960.
Tiger, Lionel. *Men in Groups*. New York: Random House, 1969.
———, and Fox, Robin. "The Zoological Perspective in Social Science." *Man*, 1:75-81, 1966.
———. *The Imperial Animal*. New York: Holt, Rinehart and Winston, 1971.
Townsend, Peter. *The Family Life of Old People*. Glencoe, Ill.: The Free Press, 1957.
———, and Wedderburn, Dorothy. *The Aged in the Welfare State*. London: Bell and Sons, 1965.
Turnbull, Colin. *The Forest People*. New York: Simon and Schuster, 1961.
———. *Wayward Servants*. London: Eyre and Spottiswoode, 1965.
Turney-High, Harry Holbert. *Man and System*. New York: Appleton-Century-Crofts, 1968.
van den Berghe, Pierre L. "Hypergamy, Hypergenation and Miscegenation." *Human Relations*, 13:81-91, 1960.
———. "Institutionalized License and Normative Stability." *Cahiers d'Etudes Africaines*, 11:413-23, 1963.
———. *Race and Racism*. New York: John Wiley & Sons, 1967.
van Gennep, Arnold. *The Rites of Passage*. London: Routledge and Kegan Paul, 1960.
van Lawick-Goodall, Jane. "New Discoveries among Africa's Chimpanzees." *National Geographic*, 128(6):802-31, 1965.
———. "Mother-Offspring Relationships in Free-Ranging Chimpanzees." *Primate Ethology*. Edited by Desmond Morris. Chicago: Aldine-Atherton, 1967.
———. "The Behaviour of Free-Living Chimpanzees on the Gombe Stream Reserve." *Animal Behaviour Monographs*, 1(3):161-311, 1968.
Ware, Cellestine. *Woman Power: The Movement for Women's Liberation*. New York: Tower Publications, 1970.
Washburn, S. L. "Behavior and the Origins of Man." *Proceedings of the Royal Anthropological Institute*, 3:21-27, 1967.
———, and Jay, P. S., eds. *Perspectives on Human Evolution*. New York: Holt, Rinehart and Winston, 1968.
Washburn, S. L., and De Vore, I. "Social Behavior of Baboons and Early Man." *Viking Fund Publications in Anthropology*, 31:91-105, 1961a.
———. "The Social Life of Baboons." *Scientific American*, 204:62-71, 1961b.
Westermark, Edward A. *The History of Human Marriage*. New York: Macmillan, 1902.

Bibliography

Whiting, Beatrice B., ed. *Six Cultures: Studies in Child Rearing.* New York: John Wiley & Sons, 1963.

Wilensky, Harold L. "The Uneven Distribution of Leisure." *Social Problems*, 9(1):32-56, 1961.

_____. "Work as a Social Problem." *Social Problems, A Modern Approach.* Edited by Howard S. Becker. New York: John Wiley & Sons, 1966.

Williams, Sharlotte Neely. "The Limitations of the Male/Female Activity Distinction among Primates." *American Anthropologist*, 73:805-6, 1971.

Wilson, Monica. *Good Company, A Study of Nyakyusa Age-Villages.* London: Oxford University Press, 1951.

Wolff, Kurt. *The Biological, Sociological and Psychological Aspects of Aging.* Springfield, Ill.: Charles C Thomas, 1959.

Wynne-Edwards, V. C. *Animal Dispersion in Relation to Social Behavior.* New York: Hafner, 1962.

Yoshiba, K. "Local and Intertroop Variability in Ecology and Social Behavior of Common Indian Langurs." *Primates.* Edited by P. Jay. New York: Holt, Rinehart and Winston, 1968.

Zuckerman, S. *The Social Life of Monkeys and Apes.* London: Kegan Paul, 1932.

Index

Aberle, D. F., 16
Abolitionism, 106
Age, absolute, 76
    chronological, 77
    relative, 76
    sociological, 77
Age grades, 17, 18, 29, 75-88, 117
Age sets, 75-88
Age stratification, 77-79, 82-88
Aggression, 24, 29, 30, 47, 48
Albania, 107
Altmann, S. A., 20
Anderson, B., 117
Andes, 54, 55
Androgen, 45
Anlagen, 43, 45, 49
Apes. *See* Primates
Arabs, 54, 58, 62, 69
Ardrey, R., 29, 30
Aristophanes, 105
Aron, R., 101

Baboons, 20-25, 28
Bacon, M. K., 47
Barry, H., 47
Basal metabolism, 42
Bascom, W., 64
Berdache, 58
Bernardi, B., 84
Biology, 1, 6-10, 33-51
Biosociology, 34

Bisexuality, 58
Blacks, North American, 89, 98, 109
Bolshevik Revolution, 106, 112, 120
Bowlby, J., 27, 32, 54
Bridewealth, 61, 71
Briggs, L. C., 61, 62
Buddhism, 57

Cannibalism, 35-36
Cannon, W. B., 36
Carpenter, C. R., 15, 16
Catherine the Great, 53
Ceylon, 53
Chiapas, 80
Child, I. I., 47
Childhood, 40, 57
Chimpanzees, 18-20, 27, 28, 29, 35
China, 59, 107, 120
Christianity, 57, 69, 70, 87
Chromosomes, 40-41
Clark, M., 117
Cleopatra, 53
Conflict, age and sex, 98-103
Congo, 73, 95
Couvade, 54
Critical period. *See* Imprinting
Crook, J. H., 13, 25
Cumming, E., 115, 116

137

Dahomey, 53
D'Andrade, R. G., 47, 55
Darwinism, 2
Davenport, R., 14, 58
De Groot, J., 50
Denham, W. W., 14
Descent, rule of, 61, 62, 67
De Vore, I., 20, 72
Diamond, M., 48
Dimorphism, sexual, 7, 14, 42-43, 56, 59, 61
Domestication of women, 90, 92
Dominance, 17, 25, 26, 52, 53, 60, 91, 92
Dumas, A., 105

Ecology, 26, 34
Economic activity, 66, 71-73
Eisenstadt, S. N., 82
Elizabeth, Queen, 53
Ellefson, J., 15
Ember, C. R., 72
Ember, M., 72
Endogamy, 93, 96
Engels, F., 4, 71
Enlightenment, 106
Environmentalism, 2
Estrogen, 45, 50
Evans-Pritchard, E. E., 58
Evolution, biological, 2, 4, 6-10, 11, 12, 26, 60
Exogamy, 93, 96

Family. *See* Marriage
Fecundity, 9-10
Foner, A., 36, 37
Fox, R., 5, 26, 46, 47, 60
French Revolution, 106, 120
Freud, S., 46, 98, 111
Frisch, J., 14
Fulani, 63
Functionalism, 2

Gahuku, 100
Gartlan, J. S., 13, 14, 25
Generation, 76-77, 102
Genes, 40-41
Genotype, 41

Germany, 107
Gerontocracy, 87
Gibbons, 15, 26
Gonads, 45
Gorillas, 16-18, 19, 25
Gouldner, A. W., 67, 68, 72
Great Britain, 54, 106, 107
Greece, 53, 58, 90
Gross, E., 108, 109

Halloween, 100
Hamburg, D. A., 46, 48, 50
Harlow, H. F., 27, 35, 47
Harlow, M. K., 27
Harvard University, 75
Hatshepsut, 53
Hausa, 61, 63-64
Hemispheric dominance, 40
Henry, W. E., 115, 116
Hermaphroditism, 6
Hinduism, 93, 96
Holter, H., 105
Homans, G. C., 98
Homeostasis, 9, 36
Homosexuality, 57-59
Hormones, 45, 50
Humor, 101
Hunting, 54
Huron, 35

Ideology, 52, 106, 107, 112, 119-120
Imprinting, 27, 34
Incest taboo, 3
India, 53, 93, 95
Inequality, 52, 77, 78, 79, 80, 91-94, 96-98, 104-120
Infant dependency, 8-9, 19, 20, 24, 27
Intelligence, 37-38, 49-50
Islam, 61, 62, 63, 65, 69
Israel, 53, 54, 56, 105
Itani, J., 21

Japan, 58, 105, 107, 113
Joan of Arc, 58-59
Job discrimination, 108-111
Johnson, V. E., 46

Index

Kamba, 82
Kawai, M., 16
Kawamura, S., 14
Kenya, 83
Kibbutz, 56
Kikuyu, 82, 84
Kinsey, A. C., 46
Kipsigi, 82
Klamath, 42
Klopfer, P. H., 29
Kohlberg, L., 47
Kortland, A., 18, 19
Kummer, H., 14, 20, 22, 23, 24, 25, 28, 30

Lactation, 9
Language, 1, 34, 40, 47, 74
Learning, 13, 28, 38, 39
Lehrman, D. S., 33
Lenneberg, E. H., 34, 40, 48, 74
Lévi-Strauss, C., 93
Lhote, H., 61
Lineages, 61, 62, 79-82
Lloyd, P. C., 64, 65
Lorenz, K., 5, 30, 33
Lunde, D. T., 46, 48, 50
Luxembourg, R., 106

Macaca fuscata, 21
Maccoby, E., 48, 49
Maclean, P. D., 26
Maria Theresa, Empress, 53
Marriage, 62, 63, 64, 65, 66, 68-71, 92-93, 95, 111, 112, 117
Marx, K., 71, 72
Masai, 83-88, 101
Mason, W. A., 14, 29, 30
Masters, W. H., 46
Matriarchy, 53, 67
Maya, 80
Mead, M., 47, 53, 118
Melanesia, 58
Menstruation, 50, 59
Meru, 82
Mexico, 80, 106
Michel, L., 106
Mill, J. S., 102
Miller, R. E., 14

Mischel, W., 47, 48
Mitchell, J., 112-113
Mitosis, 6
Mizuhara, K., 16
Molière, 105
Monastic orders, 57
Money, J., 34, 43, 45, 46, 48, 50
Monkeys. *See* Primates
Morgan, L. H., 53
Morris, D., 12, 21
Morris, R., 12
Murdock, G. P., 68

Nandi, 82
Napier, J., 12
New Guinea, 53, 100
Nigeria, 55, 63-67
Nuer, 82
Nyahyusa, 58, 85
Nyerere, J., 88

Oestrus, 46-47
Orangutan, 14
Orwell, G., 120

Papio hamadryas, 12, 13, 21-25, 28
Parthenogenesis, 6-7
Pascal, Blaise, 5
Persia, 69
Peru, 54
Peterson, R. A., 67, 68, 72
Phenotype, 41
Pleistocene, 72
Polygyny, 23, 63, 64, 68-71, 87, 92, 96, 97
Polymorphism, age, 31
Primates, 10, 11-32, 47, 60
Progesterone, 50
Prostitution, 64
Psychology, 34
Purdah, 63, 67
Pygmies, 73, 95

Racism, 2, 45, 59, 106, 119
Radcliffe-Brown, A. R., 98
Read, K. E., 100

Rebellion, rituals of, 100-101
Residence, rule of, 68
Reynolds, V., 14, 16, 18, 19
Riley, M. W., 36, 37
Rites of passage, 74-75
Rosenblum, L. A., 31
Rosow, I., 116
Rossi, A. S., 111, 112
Rowell, T., 28

Sade, D. S., 31
Safilios-Rothschild, C., 118
Sahara, 61
Scandinavia, 105
Schaller, G. B., 16, 17, 18
Schneider, D., 98
Schneirla, T. C., 131
Schultz, A. H., 15
Sears, R. R., 47, 48
Segregation, age, 116, 117
Seidman, J. M., 47
Seneca Falls Convention, 106
Senescence, 10, 36-38, 79
Seniority, 76, 78, 79, 80, 81
Sexism, 45, 106
Sex roles, 53-60, 104-113
Sexual behavior, 8, 12, 18, 20, 21, 23, 26, 46, 47, 57, 58, 59
Shanas, E., 114, 116
Shaw, G. B., 105
Shilluk, 42
Shock, N. W., 36, 37, 38
Simmons, L. W., 67
Smith, M. F., 63
Smith, M. G., 63, 64
Socialization, 57, 60, 77
South Africa, 59, 119
Southwick, C. H., 20
Soviet Union, 107, 108, 112
Speech. *See* Language
Spiro, M. E., 47, 56
Stalin, 112
Status, age, 74-88, 90-94, 113-120
    sex, 61-73, 92-94, 104-113, 118-120
Status inconsistency, 96
Stephens, W. N., 92, 93

Sudan, 61, 63
Sweden, 115

Tanzania, 58, 83-88
Technology, 72-73, 78-79, 104, 108
Territoriality, 15, 17, 29
Tiger, L., 5, 26, 46, 60
Townsend, P., 114, 115
Transvestism, 57-59
Tuareg, 61-63, 67
Tupi, 35
Turnbull, C., 73, 95
Tz'u Hsi, Empress, 53

Uganda, 54
United States, 75, 89, 90, 100, 101, 104, 106, 107, 108, 109, 110, 113, 114, 115, 116, 118, 119

van den Berghe, P. L., 100
van Lawick-Goodall, J., 16, 18, 19, 27, 28, 31

War, 53, 54
Washburn, S. L., 20, 72
Whiting, B. B., 47
Wilensky, H. L., 114
Wilhelmina, Queen, 53
Wilson, M., 58, 85

Yoruba, 55, 61, 64-67
Yoshiba, K., 14

Zuckerman, S., 12, 20, 21